SEVEN P[...]
APPLICA[...]

How to [...]
Hypnosis, Bus[...]ess, Health,
Coaching, Sport, Education
and Public Speaking

Richard Bandler
John La Valle
Anders Piper
Alessio Roberti
Alessandro Mora
Kate Benson
Garner Thomson
Owen Fitzpatrick

© Attrakt BV

IN MEMORIAM - DR RON PERRY 1952 - 2012

This book is dedicated to the great life and wonderful work of Dr Ron Perry 1952 - 2012.

We are grateful to his wife Dr Edie Perry for her commitment and drive to continue their amazing work.

'Ron has been friend, student and colleague for decades. I knew him as always curious and ready to learn. I knew Moshé Feldenkrais, one of his teachers, and I know he would have looked at Ron's work as very much a step beyond his own. He was most of all a gentle soul. This was reflected in life, and in his work. He helped me when I suffered, he made smile when I faced great adversity. He left a legacy of friends, clients, and students all the better for having known him. He day by day removed suffering from those he touched and taught all of us who listened just how it was done.

I will miss him......I find myself at a loss for words, as those who know me, this very rarely happens... ..so I will just describe him as extraordinary! I will remember always the great moments he added to my life.'

Dr Richard Bandler

IN MEMORIAM - DR RON PERRY 1952 - 2012

Dr Ron Perry will be truly missed. He was not only our friend, but he was someone who did not know the boundaries of generosity. He gave from his heart and soul. He dedicated his life to helping people be free of pain, and illness. His passion was to teach what he worked so hard to learn. Even when he was working on someone, he was using everything he knew about language and learning, to teach the person about how to use their body better. He is a tall man but he spoke and walked softly with a peace that consumed you when you met him. He was powerful and yet so gentle. He is a voracious learner and he was compulsed to be better at what he did and what he knew. He and Edie literally revolutionized what is known about chiropractics and neurology. He wove the knowledge of so many fields into what worked rather than what is traditionaly done. He is someone who will be remembered as a pioneer and forerunner in the field of healing and chiropractics. Dr Ron is a true hero among men. We will always have a place in our hearts for him and will assist in helping Edie carry on their mission of their life's work, Patterns of Physical Transformations.
We love you, Ron may your journey be blessed.

John, John Sebastian and Kathleen La Valle

Colofon

© 2012. All texts in this book are copyrighted by the respective
authors. Attrakt BV is licensed to publish these texts.

Seven Practical Applications of NLP
How to use NLP in Hypnosis, Business, Health, Coaching, Sport,
Education and Public Speaking
Authors: Richard Bandler, John La Valle, Anders Piper, Alessio Roberti,
Alessandro Mora, Kate Benson, Garner Thomson, Owen Fitzpatrick

First print: november 2012

ISBN: 9789460510700
NUR: 770

Published by Attrakt BV, Nieuwveen, the Netherlands
www.attrakt.nl

Table of contents

Introduction
Richard Bandler   6

Hypnosis as Application of NLP
Richard Bandler as interviewed by Kate Benson   8

Traits Characteristics and Behaviors of
Successful People
John La Valle   11

Applications of NLP to Public Speaking
Owen Fitzpatrick   25

The Application of NLP in Sports
Alessandro Mora & Anders Piper   38

Formatting the Brain for Healing and Health
Garner Thomson   55

NLP And Coaching
Alessio Roberti   69

Changing Beliefs
Owen Fitzpatrick & Alessio Roberti   88

Strategies for Learning
Kate Benson   98

Introduction

Richard Bandler

Hello, my name is Dr. Richard Bandler, and what we are presenting here are examples of how Neuro-Linguistic Programming applies to so many different subjects. Whether you're involved in business and the arts of persuading people, whether you are a negotiator, or you're a head hunter, whether you are involved in the educational system, or with sports athletes, whether you're involved in making presentations, or or whether you're involved in coaching, or teaching any of these skills, NLP has an application. With all of these different subjects and different aspects of life, there are workshops and trainers and authors who have written books with me or are writing books with me now. These are some, not all, but some of the top people in the field of Neuro-Linguistic Programming which unlike other fields covers everything!

Neuro-Linguistic Programming is unique in that it is not interdisciplinary but meta-disciplinary. How knowledge is formed in every field is the study of what we do. We study successful behaviors no matter what they are. To become a more successful businessman, a more successful coach, to become a more successful athlete, to become a more successful person giving presentations, a negotiator, or a hypnotist, or a neuro-linguistic programmer, all of these skills and the strategies, we've been studying for four decades only the most exquisite people who do things – art, music, poetry, architecture – because you can take the skills of a neuro-linguistic programmer and find out how these things are done – easier, better, quicker.

Our field is not about truth, it is about efficiency. This is the study of the subjective part of life, the subjective experience. Now I realize many scientists have gone off the rails and tried to make NLP scientific. It's not scientific, it's about the study of the structure of subjectivity. Language is not scientific, but yet it has rules and is rule-governed behavior. The syntax in English is different from the syntax in German and Japanese, and even though we use it and speak it as a native speaker we have no idea what the rules are, but yet we follow them. And we know when they're being followed, and when somebody's not following them.

The rules of success are no different, they're done by the most exquisite people intuitively. If you want to study the structure of success, and have the opportunity to meet the colleagues in your own field, the trainers in your own field, this Conference is a chance for me to sit down and talk to the people that have entered the field I created. To teach my own trainers to be better at what they do, my own teachers to be better at what they do, and to meet and to socialize.

It's been a long time since we've had an international meeting of the Society of NLP. We used to do this on a more regular basis, but we haven't had a chance to, for whatever reason. The chance has come and I don't know how soon it will come again. So, if I were you I wouldn't miss it, and I wouldn't miss a word in this book, or a single chance to see anyone of these exquisite teachers – read them, learn from them, go see them – it's an opportunity of a life time.

I say – move on, do your best, and then do better!

Hypnosis as Application of NLP

Richard Bandler, as interviewed by Kate Benson

KB: *Richard you are going to be teaching Hypnosis as an application of NLP on the first European Conference of the Society of NLP. Why is this such a valuable application for people to learn?*

RB: Well, just to start with, Neuro-Linguistic Programming was born out of hypnosis. When doing experimental hypnosis, I began asking the question how it is possible for people to perform tasks in a deep trance that they couldn't do in the waking state? How come a person who couldn't spell, could spell in trance or a person who had no conception of the right note in music would end up having perfect pitch when in trance. I found people could speak forwards and backwards, and as I began to ask people about how they did that, how they were capable of performing these tasks, what they described to me always came out as what initially we called a strategy.

Now once I found out the things they couldn't do in trance, I found somebody who could do it in the waking state and found out how they strategized using it. So the very tool of hypnosis removes a lot of the regular ways in which people do things, and by altering your states of consciousness, it gives you access to different capabilities in your brain.

Some of these different capabilities you find in states of age regression, some you find in states of relaxation, but getting the conscious mind and the unconscious processes of a human being lined up and aimed in the same direction is what hypnosis brought to the table.

So Neuro-Linguistic Programming became a very powerful field with very powerful tools. Now, when you turn it back the other way and look at hypnosis as an application of NLP, there are certain things in NLP that we can do better if we do them hypnotically, installation being one of the primary ones. Using belief change to induce deep trance so that you can get belief changes that last for a life time means that these two sets of skills interact. Of course, the way Neuro-Linguistic Programming does hypnosis is not the traditional form of hypnosis. We do things very differently, which allows us to do them quicker, deeper, faster, and easier.

KB: *For people who haven't experienced hypnosis, especially in the way it is taught by you and with hypnosis as an application of NLP, what are the key learnings that they will learn in this workshop?*

RB: One of the key learnings is that everybody is going in and out of trance all the time. The trick is to be able to stabilize it at just the right moment in just the right way and to be able to produce lasting change such as greater motivation.. Hypnosis is used as an amplifier, you amplify states of consciousness, you amplify the intensity of feelings, so that every tool that a 'Neuro-Linguistic Programmer' has, in fact anybody who is in the communication, training or teaching business, can be amplified in the way in which we use hypnosis.

Everything becomes more powerful when you think of hypnosis in this way, as opposed to it being about waving a watch in front of someone making them sleepy all the time! You realize that some states are of greater alertness, that you use hypnotic skills, hypnotic language patterns, and all of these things to produce magnified effects.

Traits Characteristics and Behaviors of Successful People

John La Valle
© 2012 John La Valle

Based on my experience with many different people across many different professions, the people who are the most successful have or do the following things:

- They are driven people. They are not just ambitious, they are driven by their passions, their abilities and their purpose. They know themselves so well that they do not need to explain themselves to others. Their behavior "says" it all.

- They are infectious - their drive permeates a room, permeates everyone they meet and their environment. Some people call this charisma, others energy. Whatever you call it, know what it is, because you have not only experienced it, but have it.

- They are passionate about whatever it is they do, truly passionate. Even when they have the opportunity to "sell" something, they don't have to because their passion spills over onto the people listening and/or in their presence. And most people want to have success.

- They know what that I have been saying for years. No one is good at everything, but everyone is good at something. They know what they are good at, and they have built on that. They also know what they are not good at and pass it along to someone else, when those opportunities come by.

- They know their niche and have developed their own expertise in their chosen area. They are not afraid of hard work. In fact to them it's not work. They don't equate it with their passion - to them it's not work, it's their life; it's what they love doing. As the quote says "Do what you love and you'll never work another day in your life." And at the same time, working 24/7 is part of it for them. This does not mean that they don't make time away from their "career", but there is always that one small wheel clicking away in the back of their mind that keeps them on track.

- They know that making mistakes is part of making decisions. They don't expect perfection, but they do expect optimization. At the same time, they also have high expectations for themselves, and for others, but they understand how to balance all these towards success.

- They know how to say "I don't know" with confidence. They are continuously learning, from seminars, books, tapes, etc., and from the experiences they are having. They are acute observers of their environment and can calibrate interventions well. They evaluate the results of those interventions, whether theirs or someone else's, regardless of how subtle.

- They have solid morals and values and their behavior is consistent. They do not waiver. They may change their minds, but only after very careful consideration of new information. They keep things simple - their communication, their strategies, everything possible is kept simple, but not at the expense of wasting resources, more appropriately, they keep things precise.

- They are honest and they understand dishonesty and are prepared for it. They have a healthy skepticism of the business environment in which they are operating and have the strategies to evaluate opportunities.

Now although characteristics are often thought of as innate in an individual, it is quite possible and in fact quite easy to learn the successful behavioral and language skills of NLP to begin to build success for yourself. In the rest of this chapter you will find tasters, tips and hints for some of the many attitudes, skills and behaviors of NLP utilized by successful people.

Earn the right to influence!

Too many people have a belief that they can just barge into someone's "sphere of influence", as I call it, just because of their position, or their belief in their own skills. They take their position for granted in that they somehow believe they "automatically" have the right to push people into doing things, etc. when, in fact, it doesn't quite work that way. I find in many places that "sales people", for example, are expected to be pushy, and this often prevents them from being as successful as they could be. Simply stated, they haven't "earned the right" to influence someone. Of course, personal charisma helps, but isn't the whole story.

So, how does someone "earn the right"? It starts with listening, really listening to the other person, and in such a way, that you actually do understand the other person's position, whatever it may be. This has nothing to do with empathy. When we teach people to repeat back certain key words and phrases, it's not to "mimic" the person, or just to match them to build rapport. It is because when you repeat back some of the things the other person has said, it is generated as output on your side. And in order for you to output it, you must have it encoded well enough that you also have an internal reference for it.

The side benefit is, of course, that the other person will believe that you understand them, or not, and that is highly dependent upon the quality of your output. . Earning the right means it's really a privilege.

Meta State Your Position
When you are selling and marketing your products and/ or services, one of the most important things is to have your customer, or potential customer, feel especially good emotionally about you and/or your product. Since in most cases (not all), the most powerful feelings occur in the *associated* state, it is important and useful to give the customer an experience, rather than to have them *think about* an experience. When you have your customers think about an experience, they will mostly be dissociated, which is not where you want them while *experiencing* you and/or what you are selling or marketing.

If you go on and *explain* the experience to them, much like I'm doing here, they will not necessarily have the feelings you want them to have. It's much akin to the difference between thinking about racing downhill at 80 miles per hour and racing downhill at 80 miles per hour. And the only difference, really, is the one of *perspective* -- the one you provide.

For those who may be unfamiliar with "submodalities",
here's a brief explanation. Our brains input, process
and output based on our five senses, or modalities: see,
hear, feel (both emotional and visceral), smell and taste.
Each of the modalities has other parts, hence "sub".
For example, visual includes: color or black & white; a
movie or a still shot, etc. Auditory includes: the volume;
tone, pitch, etc.

Now for those of you who are wondering about what
"meta" (going to another perceptual position), is, think
about it this way: One major position is known as
associated, that is in the experience, while the other
is known as dissociated, or being able to see/hear
yourself from the outside looking in, so to speak. There
are arguably some other positions, known as third,
etc., which are not that important for us here because
they are sub-positions of the ones just mentioned. One
of the more interesting points here, is the distinction
between *experiencing* and *intellectualizing*.

Here are some definitions from a number of sources:

Intellectualize:
1. To furnish a rational structure or meaning for.
2. To avoid psychological insight into (an emotional
   problem) by performing an intellectual analysis.
3. To examine or interpret rationally, often without
   regard to emotional considerations.

Experience:
1. The apprehension of an object, a thought, or an emotion through the senses or mind: a child's first experience of snow
2. The act of living through an event.
3. Anything or everything observed or lived through.

So, in many cases, it's sometimes necessary to go to a meta-position to detect, identify and work with submodalities, but this is highly dependent on your skill level at detecting, identifying and working with submodalities. It is not always necessary to go to another position to do any of the three.

Another distinction to make relates to which referential index to use -- I or you. Well, while this is also important, remember that "all communication is hypnosis" and the real issue is whether or not your readers will take that ride with you, even if it's yours. Can you get them excited enough using some I's and me's and some you's? That's what's going to make the difference. Using too many I's and we's will seem self serving, and too many you's may violate their rules against mind reading or patronizing.

Here is an example of text which demonstrates how to balance the use of the referential index. When I decided to publish a newsletter it was because I had so many people emailing me with the same types of questions and I found myself writing back and giving the same types of responses. And so I thought, "Hey, why not publish a newsletter? That way I can answer questions out there, and even get information out to many of the people who may not ask the questions, even though they have them. That would serve a few other purposes, then, wouldn't it?"

My first newsletter was intimidating to start with. Would they like it? Would they criticize it? Would they read it? How would I know if they like it? What if I say the wrong thing? And so many other ridiculous questions that just kept popping up. But then I thought, "Hey, what's the difference?" I mean, have you read some of the other stuff that's out there? Really! What's the worst that could happen? That someone emails me and says it sucks? Well, that has certainly happened. But the two or three we've gotten over the years are minuscule compared to the so many great complements we've got. Then I remembered my own criteria for knowing if we are doing well, or not: "Are they telling others?" Are subscriptions increasing, and what's the unsubscribe rate compared to the subscribe rate.

We have done extremely well because we've learned to listen through the years and because we have kept our promise and our schedule. It's really quite simple to do a monthly newsletter: once a month, so that you never run out of material, just often enough to maintain that presence and keep the ideas flowing amongst others. We get ideas from the people who send us questions, from our daily business activities, and from being able to laugh at the news out there. That's right, the news, high comedy! Well I'm here to tell you our subscription rate has been steady each and every week! We must be doing something right! Now every now and then, we make a mistake, but you know what? We chalk that up to experience! And we've had lots of those experiences! But it's no different than taking a chance: a trance for success!

We want to share that chance for success with YOU! From time to time, we get adventurers who submit an article for us to include in our monthly letter. Some we publish, some we don't. It really depends on how relevant it is and how much of an impact we think it could make on the lives of others! But each and every one of them has enjoyed the fact that others read their articles, and respond back to them! Every one of them has gotten responses and recognition and a boost where they need it most: in their own feel good spot! There is nothing like just putting yourself out there, taking that risk, wondering and worrying, then discovering that there are so many people out there with so many perspectives, that opportunities abound and they're FREE!! Are you ready to share in the success just waiting for YOU?

NOW, stop here and relive your experience of reading the text above. Many of you will re-experience it, some of you will *think about* it. Do both, and notice your own emotions, sensations, or lack of, those with one process versus the other. Which do you prefer and when and for what reasons? What is important here is how you can use these perceptual positions (states) in your sales and marketing.

Why - Because…. How to work THAT Meta program
Now, just in terms of sequence, remember that pacing and leading does have its value in context. And while many times, it's even OK to reverse that - to lead then pace, it's even more important to notice if you're getting the information you're seeking, or that you want or need. One of my associates noticed that his employees weren't getting the information they want from their clients, or

even potential clients. They had not yet learned to fine tune those ever valuable nuances that can make or break the day, or even the month, for that matter.

So when someone came into their studio for a workout, the client may say something like, "Hi, I decided to come in today to work out a bit." And the consultant would ask them, "Why is it important to you to work out today?" And while this all sounds well and good in context, it breaks the client's state in such a way that the consultant wouldn't get a verbal response, but would get a bewildered nonverbal response from the client. Why? Simple: the client never stated that it's important to them. And since the question is asked out of the context in which the client is operating, they would have to transderivational search beyond the first and even second derivation just to try and figure out why they are being asking this question, because of the presupposition in the question!

Now, had the consultant responded differently like this: "It's really good to see that you decided to come in today (pace) and it must be important to you that you have." And wait for the client to respond to this conversational postulate. If they say, "Yes, it is", now the consultant has the segue to go on with, "Let me ask you something, because I'm really interested in other people's motivations and reasons[1], What's important to you about that?" (Client makes submodality shift to dissociated so they can have a "better picture" and see themselves in the visual and since they're already being asked to go to a meta position to calculate what they

---

1 In fact, this is a Chialdini pattern to increase the propensity of getting a response.

are being asked to calculate, anyway, give them some assistance with the shift). And chances are, the client will provide more information in this instance.

Remember, elicitation ought to be designed to be well-targeted enough to elicit the information you want or need, and yet flexible enough to be changed quickly enough to still hit your mark. So it's not the metaprogram, or responses to the elicitation questions that provides the person's metaprograms, but the actual sequencing of their metaprograms as the person naturally speaks that provides more valuable information. So the real skill is in getting the person (customer, client) to speak naturally so you can track the programs and sequencing of them.

Towards and away from Strategies
Decision strategies abound, but which ones work the best? We want to again emphasize: LISTEN, LISTEN, LISTEN to your customers and/or prospective customers. Since you can use the Meta Program "Toward and Away From", also known as "Direction Sort" to build Propulsion Systems where do you get the information to use? We know that many of you get to hear about your customers' experiences with others, and maybe those others are your competitors, or may not be, but nonetheless they are competing with you for your customers' money. In other words, if you have $1,000 to spend, and your choices are to spend it on advertising or a new telephone system, you may spend it on a new telephone system. Now the advertiser is not necessarily in "competition" with the telephone equipment company. But they don't get your money when you've bought the telephone system.

There are stories upon stories that you'll hear of other people's bad experiences with others. After all, people will tell the bad stories more often than the good ones to others. And so, there will be lots of "what-not-to-do's" inside those stories. These "what-not-to-do's" are very fertile ground for you to harvest from.

Through the years I have built in a feedback mechanism for myself so that when I get information from outside myself that has to do with others, and that information (feedback) hasn't worked out well, I put the information into my "internal database" in my brain for what may not work. This does not mean it won't work. It means that it *may not* work. I then run it through my problem solving and creativity strategies for potential solutions and new choices. I have even sent my suggestions to a few of those people for whom the feedback was about, just because I thought they could use it.

So when you see or hear about another company or organization from one of your friends, and they have had a bad experience with that organization, take the information and run it through your problem solving strategy and/or creativity strategy and find out what's there. You may find that you develop some solutions for your own business (or even personal life). Then you can build these into your marketing or advertising, or selling and build propulsions for them. Propulsions are an important ingredient in the process because all decisions are made through comparison. Remember, there really are no new problems, it just seems that way to us because they are new *for us*. Haven't you ever noticed how it's almost always easier to help someone else solve "their" problems than it is for us to solve our own?

Switching Those Directions - Sequencing

One of the things you'll hear lots about in NLP is about setting direction. But I've found that while many people talk about it, most don't really know how to use it in everyday conversation. It's one of the most useful patterns to track for many different reasons. Once again it requires you to have the ability to listen, I mean really listen. Track each and every word in sequence as the speaker speaks. This is the skill that works best. Without open sensory channels, you're apt to put what *you* want in your prospect's mind without considering how exactly to make it fit in there. And if it doesn't exactly fit for them, then it doesn't exactly fit for them. Period.

So, Pure NLP® is about those fine basics, making those fine distinctions at the sensory based level, the way the originators of NLP intended. In fact, Pure NLP® is the most systemic of all, as it keeps things easy. The deep structures (internal representations) are best influenced through surface structures (sentences, utterances). Other modalities can and may be used, of course, but since what we use most in Sales & Marketing is language, both verbal and written, we'll use language for an example.

Now, let's look at something a client, or customer, may say: "I really want it, but I can't see buying it." In this example, there are 2 very critical elements in this example. The first and most critical is the sequence. When you say this sentence, notice that there is a *stop in the process* after saying it. There's no place to go from here. When you change the sequence to: "I can't see buying it, but I really want it." Notice what happens to your internal representation(s)! It leaves open the direction, a place to go to next. So, there are different ways to have the customer/client do this. One way is to tell them to tell you that they can't see buying it and listen to them finish the rest of the sequence.

The second critical element is the submodality shift opportunity in the sentence: "Can't see buying it." Again, in most cases, not all, but most, the generalization is that when associated to the image in the future, they most likely will *not* engage the activity. When they are dissociated in the future, they most likely *will* engage the activity. Most of you have heard or said, "I can't see myself doing that", as the presenting challenge. Well, if they could see themselves, they'd be doing it easily. Simple.

So, to change this, when they say, "I can't see buying it", you've got to challenge it with: having them say back to you: "I can't see myself buying it?" and let them finish the sequence. The interesting part here is that because of the submodality shift from see buying it to see myself buying it, whether they can or can't, the submodality shift happens anyway. Now the remainder of the sequence kicks in and takes over into the new direction. So, have fun with this!! And keep things easy! You'll be more successful as a result!

Decisions, Decisions
Thinking about deciding brought me to a point, actually, about the FREEDOM to decide and how much we take for granted that freedom. The last bastion of freedom we have is our minds and our ability to make choices, etc. These are rights we are all born with and are ours to use.
And, yet, there are people who still want to limit our

ability to think for ourselves and to learn for ourselves, and to use our own brains for ourselves. There are still those who want to have the control over thinking and deciding. It's one thing to make the choice to ask someone else for help, it's quite another to learn to help oneself. After all, it is your brain. NLP was developed to make it easier to learn to run your own brain, not to have someone else run it for you. NLP has taken away the mystery of how easy it is for someone to change! It was never based on theories and it is not seated in any other discipline. It is a meta-discipline, that is a discipline of disciplines.

Applications of NLP to Public Speaking

Owen Fitzpatrick

© 2012 Owen Fitzpatrick

They say that public speaking is the number one fear that people have, even above death. As Jerry Seinfeld pointed out... that means that, at a funeral, people would prefer to be the ones in the coffin than the one standing up giving the eulogy. It is obvious that many people suffer from a huge fear of public speaking. Speaking in front of a room full of people confidently and keeping them engaged is a skill, an art-form. In order for you to speak in public, effectively, there are three important areas you must focus on.

First, you have to be in the very best possible state you can be in. You have to have the very best attitude required to stand up in front of a room and establish credibility, attention and register interest.
Second, you have to know how to structure your speech. What are the keys to preparing and delivering a compelling speech?
Last, you have to understand the keys to winning over an audience, regardless of size. That means having a good insight into the skills that world class speakers use to win their audience over during their talks and speeches.

In order to tackle each of these areas, we will be drawing from some of the best tools that you can learn from NLP. What are the things to keep in mind and things to do in order to be at your best? We will look at presentations from three perspectives: Attitude, Actions and Abilities.

Attitude

First, let's look more closely at the attitude of world class speakers. The very best speakers feel comfortable in front of their audience. In certain situations they might feel adrenaline pumping but they interpret that as excitement and as a sign that they are looking forward to giving the presentation. The very best speakers know what they are talking about and know that they are there for one reason.... to impact the audience. This is probably the biggest difference between confident and nervous speakers. Nervous speakers have their attention focused on themselves and what the audience thinks about them. Confident speakers are focused on the audience and what the audience needs to know, understand, feel, believe or learn.

Probably one of the most important things I ever learned from Richard (Bandler) was the critical need for you to be in the best state possible. Initially, I was under the impression that the only reason why this was important was so you could feel confident enough to talk to other people. I soon learned from him that, instead, it's actually largely about how you impact other people with your state so a really big reason to control how you feel is that will control how the other person feels. The stories Richard uses are designed to not only get you fascinated and intrigued but to motivate you, help you feel confident and sure of yourself. They enable you to feel blissfully happy and ready to take on the world. It is this attitude that ensures that you can be at your best when you need to.

Focusing on the audiences state and how your state is contagious changes the frame for you and makes it easier for you to access the right kind of feeling. When your focus is on the audience you are absorbed in doing the best job you can rather than trying to impress or show off. This one distinction is hugely important. Whenever I work with someone to help them to change the way they feel about speaking in public the very first thing that I want them to understand is this.

The second thing I want them to know is that they are the ones in control. A few years ago in the Irish Management Institute I worked with a lady on stage when giving a talk on presentation skills. The lady had a phobia of speaking in public. When I asked her what specifically scared her the most, she said 'I hate being out of control and having all those people staring at me'. What I did was I helped her understand that the reality was, actually, she was the one in control when she stepped on stage. When she stood beside me I said to her 'Watch this' and I turned to the audience. I said to them 'Could everyone please stand up?'

They stood, some reluctantly, and then I continued. 'Could you please put your left arm out in the air and with your right arm touch your nose and lift your right foot 6 inches off the ground? Now please stay that way.' Once again they obeyed at which point I turned to her and said... 'Look at how ridiculous they look. When you're the speaker they will do what you say. You are in control'. That one insight added to her confidence massively and she reported that it made a big difference to how she felt on stage. When you are speaking to an audience you control their attention and you dictate what they are to do. Remembering that can help you to feel far more confident as a presenter.

The next realization to come to when you consider public speaking is that people want you to succeed when you are up there. Often when you look out at an audience they can seem ridiculously scary. But the truth is most people's concentration face involves some form of frowning. Accepting this means that you can see behind the frowns that there are smiles just waiting to happen. One good trick I've learned is that when I get up in front of an audience I always imagine the audience smiling inside their mind and my job is to make the smiles visible on their faces. Even if I don't manage it with everyone, it serves to ensure my focus is in the right place.

I have got advice before that the key is to imagine everyone naked. I don't recommend that at all. I've found you don't know where to look and if you end up staring at someone you get embarrassed quite easily! Also, another piece of advice I got was to imagine everyone as a clown. Again, it's not my favorite piece of advice. Seeing a bunch of clowns in the audience is far more scary in my opinion!

So, being confident is obviously important. But what other states are important feelings to have when you are presenting? To me, there are four key states: Power, Playfulness, Presence and Passion. The best speakers entertain and when you think about the most charismatic presenters the world has ever seen they all share either a powerful form of passion or playfulness when they talk to an audience. From the evil Hitler to the wonderful Martin Luther King, passion is an essential quality in their presentations. When you see top celebrities, television presenters or comedians playfulness is a core ingredient of what makes them absorbing to watch. When you see spiritual gurus and shaman delivering their sermons or meetings, presence is very apparent. All great speakers come across as confident and powerful in the delivery of their message.

Creating these states can involve using some state management skills that we referred to earlier. By using the Charismatic Squared exercise, you can ensure that you are accessing the very best states possible when you most need them.

Charismatic Squared

1 Think of a situation where you would like to feel and act brilliantly.
2 Think about the 4 different states (power, playfulness, passion, presence) you'd like to be feeling in that situation.
3 Imagine yourself standing in a square in front of you filled with your favorite color in the state of power or confidence.
4 Close your eyes and step into your imaginary self in the square.
5 See what you'd see, hear what you'd hear, feel what you'd feel and intensify the state.
6 Feel the feeling increase and multiply itself by itself as the color of the square gets stronger and you feel it immerse you.
7 Step out of the square and think of something else.
8 Repeat Steps 3 to 7 with power and playfulness.
9 Repeat Steps 3 to 7 with power, playfulness and passion.
10 Repeat Steps 3 to 7 with power, playfulness, passion and presence.

11 Imagine yourself in the situation from Step
1. Imagine yourself going through the once
challenging experience and step into your square.
12 Notice how much better you feel and go through
the same experience with the new feelings of
charisma.

Actions

Once your attitude is taken care of the next step is to
understand what you should be doing before, during
and after a speech or presentation. I want to offer you
a process or checklist that will come in handy for any
and every presentation you will have. This process will
ensure that you know how to plan, prepare and present
your talk in the most effective way.

Before any speech here are the things to do in order to
prepare for it.
10 Core Questions to ask before any speech to prepare
yourself adequately:

- What do they believe now about you, and the speech
  topic?
- How will they be feeling?
- What do they want from the speech?
- What qualities are important to them to have in a
  speaker, and about the topic?
- What do they do and how can the speech help them?
- Why should they listen to you?
- What do you want them to believe?
- How do you want them to feel?
- What do you want them to know?
- What do you want them to do?

The Structure of a Speech works like this:

Introduction
- Grab Attention
- Introduce Idea(s)
- Pace Audience
- Answer why they should listen
- Build States (curiosity, interest, fascination)

Body
- State the Idea(s)
- Give Examples
- Defend the Idea(s)
- Repeat the Idea(s)
- Build States (Desire, Motivation, Happiness, Confidence)

Conclusion
- Review Idea
- Review Importance of Idea(s)
- Build States (Motivation, Go for it)
- Finish Memorably

The Primacy Effect is a law in Psychology that suggests that people tend to remember best what they heard first in a presentation. The Recency Effect suggests that people tend to remember what they heard last in a presentation. Because of this, it is important that your introduction and conclusion are strong and memorable and make the point of the speech clear and concise. The old advice given on the structure of any speech is that in the Introduction you tell them what you are going to tell them; in the body tell them; in the conclusion tell them what you told them. To me, this simple strategy is a nice basic approach but there are a few other things that you need to do. For example, in the introduction it's a good idea to start with something that grabs their attention.

It's also smart to pace the audience by setting the scene and explaining what they are already thinking. Doing so allows you to create credibility because you seem to be reading the minds of those you are speaking to. Someone who does this really, really well is Kathleen La Valle. I remember struggling with the concept of the Meta Model years ago and sitting in on a session where she was teaching it. After the first few minutes of her speaking, before we even explored the first pattern, I was already feeling far more confident about it. I remember having a kind of light-bulb moment when it seemed like she knew exactly what was on my mind. Feeling that made it so that when she explained it, for the first time, it really made sense. (it also helped that the explanation was really clear as well!)

Another important thing to do at the beginning of a talk is to explain why they should listen to you. By giving them a reason you heighten their motivation and make it more likely that they will pay attention to you. When teaching any concept or idea you have to explain why it's a useful thing for them to know. You have to make it clear that there is a really good reason for them to pay attention to you. It doesn't matter if you have the secrets of the universe to tell people, if you don't let them know then you won't have their attention. I used to think that this wasn't that important. I used to pride myself in being able to explain complicated ideas in simple ways and quickly and easily. Then I realized that when other trainers or speakers would spend a lot of time on one simple technique, it gave more value to that technique in the mind of the audience. So, by me taking the technique for granted so would they and they wouldn't necessarily realize just how effective and powerful the technique really was. Nowadays, although I still keep things simple, I make sure that I emphasize the value of what they are going to learn before I teach it.

During the speech, here are the key things you need to do. It's important to walk and talk with confidence and purpose from the time you walk on the stage until the time you walk off it. Your body language sends signals to your brain and the brains of others about you as being a confident and credible person. Literally, chemicals are released in your brain whenever you walk in a confident way that actually makes you feel more confident. Similarly, when your posture is bent over and stressed, chemicals are released in your mind that makes you feel stressed and worried. Make sure that you walk and stand how you want to feel. Next, manage your energy and stay vibrant. It's essential that you learn to stay present and be full of energy when you deliver a presentation. A lot of people overlook this because they are too focused on the content of their presentation. But unless you can engage people properly your content won't matter.
Just as important as that, it's a good idea to tune into the energy of the audience you are speaking to and prepare some energy boosters or audience engagement techniques for when their energy drops. That means even in a speech, it's a good idea to get the audience doing something. Demonstrations on

stage, exercises, group discussions are all ways that keeps their energy level high. Another important essential to bare in mind is to stay on track throughout. Keep everything relevant to the presentation and to the audience and keep answering the question 'Why should they care?' as you explain the ideas you are speaking about.

After the speech, here is a process to make automatic. Collect whatever feedback you can get on how you did and find out what you can do to improve. If possible, collect footage of the speech so you can go back and watch it and dissect it so you can learn from it. Immediately afterward when you get a chance mentally review the speech in your mind and ask yourself where there is room for improvement and what you did particularly well. Learning from your presentations is one of the behaviors that marks the greatest speakers out from everyone else. Also allow yourself to bask in the glow of a good presentation. It's important to get to enjoy presenting as much as possible and one of the best parts is the fantastic feeling you get after a speech goes great. In the event it doesn't go well, just immediately ask what can you learn from it and then move on.

Abilities
Last, there are a number of skills that come in handy when you are speaking in Public.
First, reading the audience means paying attention to their responses to whatever you are saying. Some humor will work, some won't. Some stories will make an impact. Some won't. Some ideas will stick in their mind. Some won't. By paying attention to them you will

start to notice what topics interest them the most and what don't. You will learn what to put more emphasis on and what to ignore. Even in big audiences, you will be able to see when they start getting tired and wandering off and that's the time to change the tempo or do an exercise. All presentations should be two way. It's the only w ay you can be sure to get them paying attention to you.

Another skill is to use language skills such as Truisms and Presuppositions. Both of these are explained in the chapter on Changing Beliefs. The reason they are so important is that truisms are one of the best resources you have to create rapport with a big group. Since it's not as easy to pace them through your body language, the key is to pace them through language itself as you can often predict things you know that is true for the audience or group that you are speaking to. By saying what they are thinking you will boost your credibility in their mind and ensure that they are more likely to be influenced by you.

Being clear and giving concrete and specific examples is another really important part of making presentations. All too often, people talk in high level concepts. This is especially true in the business world. People use terms like 'Productivity' and 'Sustainability' without ever being clear over what they are talking about. When you give a specific real example, for example, a client called Barry that you worked with on managing his time because he missed his ten year old son David's birthday, it makes the example feel more real than 'I worked with a client with time management issues'. This is one of Richard's secrets. He uses the actual cases of real clients he's worked with and describes them vividly which makes his stories so absorbing. Using Humor is a really good idea if you want to be an engaging public speaker. We all know how funny the best NLP trainers out there like Richard and John (La Valle) are... but even outside of NLP, other world class speakers utilize humor on a regular basis. The reason that they do is simple. When you make people feel good they enjoy listening to you. Not only that but they are far more likely to remember what you said. The kinds of chemicals released when a person laughs improve the likelihood that they will remember whatever they're hearing at that moment in time.

Public Speaking and making presentations for many can be the hardest thing that people do. In reality though, once you change your attitude and state and you learn the actions and abilities of the best speakers, it really does become something that can be mastered. You will always learn and I still learn from the great speakers and trainers out there including the fantastic speakers at this conference, They all have different styles and I think one of the best skills you can have is to watch others and understand what you can take from them. Kate, for example, has a massive amount of experience in Education and there is a difference between teaching and training. Although a great trainer, Kate brings in subtle skills from teaching that many people don't know which is really interesting.

Other sources of great presenters would be well known motivational speakers like the late, great Jim Rohn. Another would be Zig Ziglar. There are incredible politicians that we can learn from. My training partner in Ireland and the other half of the Irish Institute of NLP, Brian Colbert, for example, has a very distinct style and is one of the best I've seen in action and as we often co-train together and can finish each other's sentences, This gives me a great opportunity to watch him in action on a regular basis.

By learning from great presenters such as these, I get to continuously refine my presentations so that I can make more of an impact. It's about ensuring you have the best possible attitude, take the best possible action and learn the best abilities. When you do that, you will be a cut above the rest. The most important thing though, out of everything, is to make sure that you practice what you learn. That will be the difference between those that present like a champion and everyone else.

The Application of NLP in Sports

Alessandro Mora & Anders Piper
© 2012 Alessandro Mora & Anders Piper

Lots has been said and done in the pursuit of victory. Many times we have witnessed underrated athletes or teams succeed and favorites or dream teams fail. In the world of sports, the word performance has so much more to it compared to so many other contexts. In the game of soccer, with 11 players on the field from each team, no one team will win just because they have one star, and the team won't necessarily win just because they have 11 stars playing on the same side.

In American Football a quarterback who can run and pass, isn't necessarily the best in the league. If he doesn't have the skills to tie his offense together or if the rest of his offense isn't up to his speed, they won't score. Bicycling is an interesting sport, performed by individuals in a team. So arguably there is some kind of team effort but at the end of a grueling 8 hour race, when all muscles ache, when the body is tormented, what is it that makes the athlete able to dig in deeper and push through that pain, so much more than the rest? In a marathon race, when the body is totally depleted of its resources and yet keeps going or in an ultra-run, perhaps 100km or more, how can the athlete continue?

What is it that makes the great athletes or the great teams win? What is it that makes teams of great athletes fall apart from time to time? And how can you take greatness in individuals and merge that into a winning team formula? What is the real difference between talent and greatness? What is the real difference between Champs and Chumps?

When you think about application of NLP in sports, a whole wonderful world appears and a lot of interesting things begin to happen. Different types of sports have different challenges. Team sports have different issues than individual sports. And individual sports have different issues when you're competing against an opponent who is trying to make your life harder (tennis, bicycling, all the fighting sport, car racing, cross country, swimming etc.) or when you are competing mainly against yourself and you are in principle the only one who can destroy your own game (in disciplines like shooting, archery, golf, figure skating, high jump, pole jump, gymnastics, alpine skiing, etc). We have always loved working with athletes and teams because you can immediately see the results of your work. In fact there is always a match, a race, a game or a practice day where you have the possibility to test if you have done a good job with your athletes or if you have to do something else.

Why is NLP and mental training skills are so important in sports? Probably you've noticed athletes (maybe even yourself) having some "magic" days, when everything you do comes easily: you score, jump, bat, block, skip, shoot, swing, etc. perfectly and you're unstoppable. Those are great days when you're in the flow, in the zone. And we are also sure you've noticed the "other" days, when everything is going in the wrong direction. Even the simplest thing that you do everyday seems to be the most difficult task in that precise moment. The part that always amazed both of us, is that sometimes, between these two completely different situations is just a matter of hours… or even minutes!

How can it happen? You are the same person, with the same resources… what makes the difference? Think about it for a minute. Is it possible that athletes forgot their knowledge or the ability to perform a gesture or a technical skill? Is it possible that in two following days (or hours) your physical shape could change so dramatically? From your own personal sport experience or simply by using your logic, I'm sure your answers to these questions are "no". So again: what makes the difference?

The two traditional key factors for the peak performance
Let us back up a little bit. In the history of every sport the first aspect that every athlete (with their coach) practices every day is the technique: they focus on learning and fine tuning those technical skills that will allow them to maximize their performance and win the game. They plan, they practice their routine, they have a performance model, etc… everything that can be useful to acquire perfectly the skills they need. And together with the technique, another important aspect is trained every day in almost every sport: the tactics. It means how to utilize in a strategic way their abilities to win upon a specific opponent. For example if the opponent team plays with a specific module, the coach will "position" his players in order to maximize their strengths and minimize their weaknesses. And here it comes all the different modules, strategies, scouts with statistics, video supports, etc.

And that's perfect! Technique and tactics are very important in every sport, and that's why you practice those everyday. Then, after a while, sports people realized that those technical and tactical skills alone weren't enough. You could be the "best" player in the world, but if you run less, if you jump lower, if you have less resistance, you will finish behind the ones who have more fuel.

This was the beginning of the "physical training era", when athletes started methodically training their body. And everybody could see the results. If you watch Roger Federer, Rafael Nadal or Novak Djokovic playing a tennis match, you can immediately notice two big differences compared to the champions of the 80's: the speed and the power! And this is the result of a specific and high level physical training. One very recent and very good example of this is the winner of the 2012 Tour de France, Bradley Wiggins. His physical training is so systematic that it would kill most people mentally, but it gives him the strength to go that extra mile. As an example, after a long stage, he will go on the stationary bike and do 45 minutes of specific training, designed to stimulate the recovery of his muscles... at this time his competitors are all back at the hotel getting their massage.

Even those who play professional golf (which at a first look doesn't seem the most strenuous sport) take their time to go to the gym and build muscles: in fact if you hit the ball harder, it goes further and you start cutting strokes. You can go to Tiger Woods official website[1] and see his all round conditioning program, to get an

1 Cf. http://web.tigerwoods.com/fitness/workoutRegimen

idea about what he stacks on top of the many hours of practice on the golf course.

Today almost every pro athlete or team has their physical coach, because they want to be in the perfect shape when they need it. Now imagine this: think about a final in whatever sport you like. The two athletes (or teams) are playing the last points. Technically and tactically they are phenomenal (otherwise they wouldn't be there), physically they are well trained: "So what makes the difference between who wins and who loses?"

If you ask top athletes in many different disciplines the same question, every single time the answer has to do with the same factor: the one who wins is the one who can stay more focused, the one who is not scared, the one who is not overwhelmed and can cope with pressure… the one who doesn't lose his mind and instead know how to use it for winning purposes.

So if the difference is not in the arm or the leg, not in the shear muscle mass or power, not in the equipment you have and not even in the amount of money you have access to, where is it then? The difference we are talking about is primarily the combination of the mind and the heart running all the above mentioned things! It is how you think and feel about your game that makes the difference and we know that if the mind and heart isn't there, you risk losing your game! So the big question is: how come that many athletes still do not spend as much time on this part of their game as with the other parts.

Start training the third factor for peak performance: the "Invisible Skill"

And then that brings another interesting question to our mind: "If technique and physique are well trained everyday… then what about the mind, what would happen if you started training the mind everyday?"

What we're talking about here is the "invisible skill" that allows you to express your potential at the maximum level. Well, you need to practice this skill. The reason why it's called mental training or conditioning and not mental "miracle" is because the key word is TRAINING: training your mind to play with you and not against you. And, like all the other skills, the more you practice, the more you will be in control when you need it. And that's because it's your brain and you can learn how to use it! So you can use your brain for a change!

Of course there are great coaches who already uses mental training and conditioning with their players but still too few to mention. You can make the difference! Using NLP in sports can be the thing that can have a game changing influence on the way you think about your game and those strategies can help you utilize the talent and skills you have in you or on your team in a revolutionary way. NLP applied in sports can help you manifest success. No more, no less, just that!

We have divided our approach into four distinct areas, each focusing on different aspects of the mental game. The sequencing is not coincidental and you can choose to read from start to end, thus understanding what we believe is the sequence of success when working with an athlete or a team, or you can go directly to the one issue that you may already have isolated as the area where you need to focus in order to change or improve your performance.

The four areas are:
- Desired State.
- Present State.
- Limits.
- Resources.

Obviously covering all of these four areas would be more than we have space for here, so let's look at a common scenario that happens all the time and see how we can define this in NLP terms.

The mental conditioning world
In the ideal world, athletes come to us because they want to be better and perform at their best in order to win a championship, a big tournament (like the Olympic Games) or play better as a team… instead ironically most people come to us when things go wrong and they don't know what to do next: they lost their swing, their game became poor, they can't perform anymore at the level they are supposed to belong…
… and in those circumstances they usually start telling themselves stupid things like "I'm not good enough", "I can't do it anymore", "everything is going wrong", "I'm too old", etc. and the worst part is that they start believing it. And this could be the beginning of the end… or the beginning of our job.
So although we would like to start somewhere else, usually our job begins here. This is where we start:

1: Beliefs

Probably you've already heard Henry Ford's famous quote "If you think you can do something or you think you can't, you're right". What you believe to be true gives you the power engine to create your result (or, on the other hand, it can stick a person at the starting blocks). Who thinks small, probably will get small results… but when you start thinking big, something extraordinary happens.

During the last Olympics in London, something kept our attention. It was a 21 years old boy from Guatemala called Erik Barrondo. Honestly until that race we didn't know him, but we loved this story when we heard about it. Before Erick Barrondo traveled to London to compete at the Olympics, he bought his family their first-ever TV. Good decision. In fact his parents could watch him race in the 20-kilometer walk in which he won a silver medal. It was the first medal of any color at any Olympic Games for his nation.

But this is not the best part. After the extraordinary result, during an interview, Erick said: "We do not have a good financial situation, but I made an effort and bought a TV for my parents". And when his father objected that there were more important things to buy before a television, the young athlete replied: "Dad, I want you to see me win a medal, I have faith in winning".

If we could talk to him, we would ask: "how do you know you will win a medal?", "can you see yourself?", "how specifically? Is that a movie of the race or you can see yourself on the podium after the race?". The answers to these kind of questions reveals his subjective way of thinking about the race and about winning the medal. It gives us his "winning mentality".

Now, when you discover how a person specifically thinks about something he knows he can do greatly, you do 2 steps:

1 notice the most important piece of all: people think about these great experiences (WOW) in a completely different way than those experiences in which they think they are not good enough (boo).

2 take all the "challenges" he has and help him to think about those in the same specific way he thinks about what he knows he can do greatly (WOW)

When we speak about "the way", the same concept that exists in NLP, we are talking about the structure (and not the content). You want to know the pictures they have in their mind as they think about those WOW experiences, the sounds they hear, what they tell to themselves, the feelings attached to it… even the smell or the taste if it's in their thinking. The more accurate the representation they give to you about those experiences, the simpler it will become in helping them to set a winning attitude: they already have inside them all the resources they need to peak perform.

"If you can dream it you can do it!"

Walt Disney

When your conscious and unconscious mind is aligned on the idea that you can do it, you need to access your resources. Remember: athletes (especially top athletes) already can peak perform. They just need to learn how to get into that particular state (or series of states) that allow them to use those extraordinary resources and skills. This is known as the state of "flow", which is when you are in the zone. And every athlete needs to learn how to create it on purpose, when he wants it. This is the second key for the peak performance:

2: State Management

You've heard it so many times from people in the world of sports: "I was in the zone." Well, as we already said the idea of being in "the zone" is defined as being in Flow. Flow is the optimal experience and condition. This is that very moment when you are challenged in a way where there is a balance between challenge and/or requirements on one side and your skill and resources on the other. It is a state of mind; it is in that state where we experience the Optimal Experiences.

Optimal Experiences are the moments where, instead of letting yourself be controlled by blind forces, you feel in control of your own actions and destiny. Those rare occasions where you are caught by a feeling of excitement, a feeling of happiness, which you can treasure for a long time and which will stay in your memory as expressions of how life ought to be. These are moments where nothing else matters and you become so absorbed in what you do, just because you enjoy doing it. These best moments in our life are not passive, receptive or relaxed. We have worked hard for them. They typically comes when our body or mind are stretched to the limit in an attempt to achieve something difficult and valuable. So we can say that

Optimal Experiences is something we make happen! Optimal Experience is the result of development and every single person has thousands of possibilities and challenges that can serve as development!

So being in the Zone or in Flow is a state of Optimal Experience and from the original work with it we know that the formula for Flow requires the following in order to happen:

1 Create a compelling goal and make the appropriate number of realistic sub-goals (Milestones)
2 Find ways to measure progress according to the chosen goals
3 Concentrate on what you are doing and constantly raise challenges that the activity gives you
4 Develop the necessary skills that makes you able to do the activity
5 Keep raising the stakes if the activity starts to bore you.

Although in the original work it was stated that this was not something you could influence yourself, we dare to differ. With the power of NLP we can easily create a process that can enhance and promote all of the above.[2] As much as we can talk about various techniques and exercises that can help get you into that wonderful state of Flow, you could also design and generate the state yourself. Wouldn't that be something?

---

2 You can read more about this in the Book 'Shortcut to Flow' by Anders Piper

Create a compelling goal and... Enjoy it more!
Now if you think back to the first steps towards Flow, you have to know where you want to go, so it is crucial that you have your goal out there in front of you in order to set a direction for yourself. Your goal should be behavior related, so that it can generate things for you, if your goal is just a 'thing' it may not be sustainable. Once you know what you want in terms of behavior, then this requires you to be in a certain state of mind and why not attempt to be in Flow as much of the time as humanly possible? Once you know what you want, then you can ask yourself "If I am really enjoying this activity, what and how would that feel? What would be the components that make up this feeling?

Once identified, there are several ways of generating that feeling. You can stack or chain the various states that make up this new and powerful state or you can spin the various states into each other, thus generating a new wonderful feeling representing the state you want to be in. In any case, you can easily identify the ideal state to be in, that can support you in achieving excellence and peak performance. These two skills are the basis on which you can build your work as an athlete or as a sport coach. The direction you take and the techniques you will use depend on the athletic goals.

What makes a team?
Another question is: what happens when more than one person is involved and you have to deal with a team? In Europe one of the best leagues in Soccer is the Premier League in England and yet as a national team, they haven't done well in years, despite teams

like Manchester United, Chelsea, Arsenal, Liverpool etc. Now you may say that it's the foreign players making the league great, but in most cases it works the other way around. The great player's wants to play in great leagues, so arguably perhaps the Premier League is only surpassed by the Primera Division in Spain (sorry Italy and Germany and all the other great leagues).

Again, what are the differences between a great team and a collection of individuals that are supposed to play together? Once a player (in any level of his or her sport) reaches a certain level that separates them from the rest and makes them stand out, very often they start getting different treatment from the coaching staff and they start to expect different treatment. All of this develops ego. Ego is not a good or a bad thing, it's just the persona and in sports the ego often is an expression of the desire to win. It is just that there is much more of a desire in the ones that goes to the top. The desire is what makes them train harder and the desire is what makes them go that extra mile in their efforts to win a game.

As long as we are talking about individual sports this can be a very good and supporting attitude, but in team sports it can lead to failure if not handled the right way. A professional soccer player once said, that "a top soccer team consists of 25 individuals all focused on their own success and the job of the coach is to channel all of that energy in the same direction". That is exactly what we will do here and let's start with the most important step.

Creating a joint purpose

When you have a group of individual talents, all skilled and all eager to perform and show what they can do, it is of utmost importance that you can channel their energy in the same direction. Many believe mistakenly that a common goal, like a championship, will do that for the team, but this is not the case. Each player needs to understand the purpose of being on the team, they need to understand what the whole idea of being a team is all about and how each player has to contribute to that higher unit called the team.

It's the big why question, so simple, yet for many so hard to define. So let's play with an example. Let's say that the team defines the purpose as winning championships. In sports I am sure that many would say that would constitute a pretty good purpose, but what happens if we challenge that? If the team gets together with the sole purpose of winning the championship, each and every player will focus on that and it may in fact lead to a successful season with a nice trophy at the end. But how much will the star players support the new talents when it is only about this season? And without that crucial mentoring process, what then happens if or when one or more of the stars gets injured? Is there anyone to step up? Many times there isn't anyone. Of course with enough cash you can buy more talent and keep it in store, but they are not going to just sit and wait forever. Although it's nice to be part of a winning organization, for most players it is even nicer to be contributing. Many would rather have playing time for a lower ranked team than be benched or red-shirted forever.

Now if we go back to the idea of having a purpose that generates more than just short term results and we hold on to the idea of winning championships, we could add something about sustainability. So what if we say that the purpose of the team is to develop and nurture a championship organization that can go all the way? With this change in words something magic happens. We have now transitioned from the end result to the process of getting there, haven't we? If we start considering the team as an organization, things change because in any organization there are various units each with their own responsibilities and contributions. But in a successful organization people work together, because we can thrive on success for just one year, but rather we want to build a self-sustaining mechanism, that can stay on top year after year.

It is very much like a garden. If you only plan one year ahead every year your garden will not look that pretty, simple because some plants needs more time to peak and show their real beauty. Now if we hold on to the garden metaphor for a moment, you also need to water the garden and weed out some stuff from time to time in order for other plants to grow and occasionally you redesign part or whole of your garden in order to get a fresh start. Now of course in sports, it is about trophies, let's not kid ourselves! There is nothing that beats the feeling of winning. You never grow too old to enjoy winning, it's that simple, however if you have a real championship team that just wins everything, there is always a risk of complacency appearing, the "We will win no matter what" syndrome, which ever so often has led better teams to lose. Competing at a high level in any sport, requires star players but once you have a star how do you keep them there? How do you keep them motivated? Well a simple way is making sure that you always have new and upcoming stars knocking on the door, thus the idea of inserting new people to develop and nurture towards the purpose.

Now this line of thinking requires guts in the coaching staff! What do we do when we have players who do not want to focus on the team purpose? What if they don't care about the other players or don't want to mentor younger players? If we look at a team as an organization, we know that in an organization we have management and leaders, each responsible for developing and nurturing their particular department and they have job descriptions that state the responsibilities that they have and that they get measured on. How many athletes have in their contract, the responsibility of mentoring and nurturing young players? Well unofficially we have the structure with team captains and in some organizations that seems to work, but why don't we make it the official duty of any star player that it is part of their responsibility and that part of their bonus is attached to how well they perform that task?

Great coaches develop and inspire leaders just like that. Both on the field and on the coaching staff so we can see in consistently successful teams there is a spirit of passing on and mentoring but unfortunately we also see stars who act like irresponsible prima donnas, just taking care of themselves! So when you want to generate that team purpose, it is important that you think beyond just the next championship and that you look into the future you want to be having. Now of course you may define the team as a project team with the sole purpose of winning the next title and there is nothing wrong in that… but remember that this will also only produce short term results. No matter whether the focus is short or long term the purpose is all about why the team is there and describes in a short and simple sentence the process that you want everyone to focus on.

The purpose of these few pages is to instill a simple idea: there's a lot to do in the sports environment working with mental conditioning. You can work with the single athlete, the whole team and eventually staff, managers and the whole organization. Our focus is to help people to peak performance, much like the traditional sports coach. With NLP skills and techniques we have definitively the perfect set of tools to do it. So to use a well-known phrase in sports: Just Do It!

Formatting the Brain for Healing and Health

This chapter has been extracted from Magic in Practice – Introducing Medical NLP: the Art and Science of Language in Healing and Health (Revised and Updated Second Edition) and is published by permission. Copyright © 2012 Garner Thomson and Khalid Khan. All Rights Reserved.

Garner Thomson

© 2012 Garner Tomson

One of the enduring mysteries of Western medicine is why two people with apparently identical conditions and receiving exactly the same treatments or advice respond entirely differently. Just as mystifying is why so many patients seem to forget or disregard advice or treatment – even in the face of life-threatening conditions. Statistics suggest that barely half of all patients follow treatment plans and instructions. Britain's National Audit Office reports that wasted drugs alone could be costing the country up to £100 million a year[1], whereas in the United States, the cost has been estimated at more than $100 billion.[2]

Medical NLP's response to this has been to explore various means of helping the patient to improve both adherence and the effectiveness of treatment. Rather than adopting the ruling belief (that the patient needs to become aware of the gravity of his or her condition, thereby improving compliance), our focus has been on creating experience and choice for the individual.

One of the key presuppositions of Medical NLP is simple, but like many simple concepts, profound in its

---

1 Available from: www.nao.org.uk/publications/nao_reports/06-07/0607454.pdf

2 Berg JS et al (1993) Medication compliance: a healthcare problem. Annals of Pharmacotherapy 27: 1–24

implications: people often don't know how to get better. The role of a health practitioner, therefore, should not only be to deliver treatment appropriate to the patient's needs, but also to ensure that the therapeutic seeds fall on fertile ground. But, how can someone be given the "experience" of healing when healing has not yet taken place? What specifically can be done to prepare the patient for this degree of change?

What follows is a simple three-part methodology designed to improve compliance, adherence and clinical effectiveness at the level of the patient's unconscious processes.

Preparing the ground
Back in the day before SD Cards, USB memory sticks and solid-state hard drives, computer memory was expanded using 5¼-inch magnetic diskettes, widely known as "floppies". The key characteristic of these floppies was the need for formatting – a lengthy process designed to prepare the surface to receive the zeroes and ones of your computed data. If the process went as planned, the diskette could be used to store several megabytes of data (gigabytes were still the stuff of computer nerds" dreams). Sometimes – more frequently than most of us would have liked – the process failed. Bad sectors and other mysterious glitches meant you had to scrap that particular floppy and replace it with another one, at no little cost.

Human minds seem to have more in common with computational processes than most of us would care to admit. The need for "formatting" – preparing the brain to accept, store and apply new patterns – is one process now specific to all Medical NLP trainings. Our experience is: if people don't know how to do something specifically, they often won't do anything at all. Conversely, when the brain is effectively configured and the right patterns are successfully installed, health-appropriate behaviors become automatic.

But, before we look at how to "format" the mind in order effortlessly to accept new information, we need to ask: what stands in the way of people simply acting on good advice? Why can't everyone just follow instructions, or take the pills, and go on to live long, healthy and happy lives? What so often thwarts understanding and change?

A story we heard some time ago featured a gifted young medical student strolling along the banks of a river with his professor when they heard the cries of a drowning man. Being young and fit, the student leaped in and dragged the man to safety.
A few meters further along, to their surprise, they spotted another man, swept up in the current and screaming for help. Again the student plunged in to the rescue. Only minutes later, the same thing happened. The now drenched and exhausted student dragged the victim to safety, and gasped, "I don't know how many times I can keep doing this." The professor pondered for a moment and then said gently, "Perhaps you should run ahead and stop who-ever's pushing them in…"

With between a third and a half of all patients who seek medical attention suffering from symptoms that have

no identifiable pathology or cause[3][4][5] the time has come
to move upstream and take another look at the factor
or factors that all of them have in common.

A global epidemic
The feature with most impact on the patient's failure to
function optimally is undoubtedly stress. "Stress" has
been labeled a "global epidemic" by the World Health
Organization on the basis of studies showing that it
can disrupt the functioning of almost every organ and
system in the body, and is implicated to some degree
in all cognitive and emotional dis-ease. According to
the American Medical Association, stress is the cause
of 80 to 85 percent of all human illness and disease
and contributes directly or indirectly to coronary
artery disease, cancer, respiratory disorders, accidental
injuries, cirrhosis of the liver and suicide – six major
causes of death in the United States. And yet, despite
evidence for the role of stress in human illness, no
effective, comprehensive model or guidelines exist to
give practitioners the tools and understanding to curb
its impact.

The reductionist approach to illness has led inevitably
to organizing presenting symptoms into sometimes
arbitrary syndromes, which creates an illusion of
discrete conditions, each of which has (or is assumed

---

3 Olde Hartman T, Lucasseen P, Van de Lisdonk E, Bor H, Van de Weel C
(2004) Chronic functional somatic symptoms: a single syndrome? British Journal of General Practice 54: 922–7

4 Rosendal M, Olsen F, Fink P (2005) Management of medically unex-
plained symptoms. British Medical Journal 330 4–5

5 Wessley S, Nimnuan C, Sharpe M (1999) Functional somatic syndromes; one or many? Lancet 354: 936–9

to have) a single, specific cause. Treatment then tends to be proximate, aiming at the most readily identifiable co-factor to provide symptomatic relief, usually by pharmacological or surgical means.

In Medical NLP, we revisit the deeply complicated and controversial subject of stress with a view to redefining its purpose and function. We are not suggesting that all illnesses can be "cured" simply by "managing" stress. Nor are we suggesting that "learning to relax" or "changing your job" is what we mean by managing stress. In fact, what we mean by "stress" isn't even what most people mean by stress. But we, and many of our colleagues, can report considerable success in helping patients learn to understand the "purpose" of their symptoms, and to master newer and more creative means of responding to them, thereby gaining real control, and often, complete recovery from many chronic disorders which otherwise frustrate the health professions.

The freeze response
One of the responses associated with unprocessed stress, or autonomic overload, is what Medical NLP practitioners call "limbic hang-up". This is an involuntary shift in cognitive processing that takes place when the subject is under pressure and corresponds to the "freeze" state of the fight-flight-freeze response to physical and emotional challenge. In evolutionary terms, it's easy to see that the response is adaptive. Whether you're stepping into your morning shower, driving to work in the morning rush hour or facing a tiger that's escaped from the zoo, your brain is working at near light-speed to monitor for potential threats, mobilize your resources and prompt you to action.

Responding to millions of years of natural selection, your brain "remembers" the dangers of confronting a predator without full preparation. The protective regions of your limbic brain are ancient and quick-tempered. They mistrust the slower calculating speed of the more "reasonable" frontal cortex. The quarter-second or so that it takes to assess a situation rationally may mean the difference between life and death, so, if the alarm is strident enough, it hijacks activity away from rational thought and entrusts your survival entirely to a primeval, entirely automated, response.

As "primitive" and out-dated as this response might seem, it is still a fully active part of the modern human brain. The problem is, that a few of the challenges we face today are truly life-or-death situations, as the limbic region is apt to believe. Subjective experience of this response is often mistaken for, and treated as, the symptom of some dysfunction or disease. Racing heart, churning stomach, tingling sensations in the fingers and feet, strange shifts in vision – these have given rise to a seller's market in drugs, ranging from anti-depressants and beta-blockers to proton pump inhibitors and simple, over-the-counter antacids. In reality, what is happening is not only natural, but highly desirable in a situation of genuine threat.

This is why:
The heart speeds up and the breathing rate increases in order to oxygenate the body, ready for action; the stomach churns as digestion is suspended and blood is pumped away from the viscera to the limbs in order to strengthen them. Vision often narrows down (if a tiger has been detected in the undergrowth, this is hardly

the time to be distracted by the bunch of ripe berries hanging just within your reach).

Neuroscientist Joseph Ledoux has proposed a model of fear-conditioning which includes a neural "high road" (including the ability to consciously process and respond to the perceived threat) and a "low road" (which includes unconscious fear responses).[6]

A "high road" response seldom causes problems. You recognize the threat, respond appropriately, and file the incident away without undue traumatic impact on the system. Physical responses (pounding heart, churning stomach) tend to subside rapidly. On the other hand, if the threat is rated as significantly life-threatening, blood pumps away from the prefrontal (rational) cortex, to the back of the brain (seat of memory, emotion and knee-jerk reaction). This saves the quarter-second or so that might be needed to rationally assess a specific situation, thus minimizing the risk of hesitation when you should be getting ready to save your life.

All in all, this "low road" response prompts you to become strong ... but you also become dumb. Furthermore, if you cannot respond by physically fighting or running away, the system simply hangs up.

Why patient's don't "listen"
Medical NLP suggests that practitioners regard all patients suffering physical or emotional distress as being in a state of limbic hang-up. It is important, then, to remember that during this neurological

6 LeDoux J (1996) The Emotional Brain: The Mysterious Underpinnings of Emotional Life, Simon & Schuster, 1998 Touchstone edition

storm, the subject, having dissociated from the more logical prefrontal cortex, is significantly less likely to be able to process input, however rational and reasonable this might be. He or she may not even properly hear what is said during the consultation. It is almost certain that most of what is said will be quickly forgotten.

Happily, the key to both identifying autonomic overload and responding to it lies in a single pattern - the patient's breath. Mainstream medicine pays little attention to breathing, except where respiratory tract or cardiac disorders are suspected. In these cases, investigation is restricted to respiratory rate, dyspnoea (difficulty in breathing), tachypnoea (unusually rapid breathing), blood oxygen saturation, breathing sound (for example, wheezing or vesicular), and recession (affected by abnormalities of the muscles of the chest wall).

The Medical NLP practitioner, on the other hand, is encouraged to be alert to:
- rapid breathing;
- upper chest breathing;
- sighing;
- sniffling;
- yawning;
- irregular breathing;
- audible breathing during rest;
- apnoea (holding the breath);
- unusual or effortful breathing, and, especially,
- breathing through the mouth.

All these behaviors result in over-breathing which forces carbon dioxide from the lungs, and strips it from blood, tissue and cells. This, in turn, prevents oxygen from being released from the hemoglobin into tissues and organs, a phenomenon first identified in the early 20th Century, and known as the Bohr Effect.[7]

A number of research projects now suggest that reduced carbon dioxide levels can cause excessive cortical excitability, resulting in anxiety[8], depression and a wide range of physical and psychological disorders. According to cardiologist Claude Lum, hyperventilation may give rise to a collection of "bizarre and often apparently unrelated" symptoms which may affect any part of the body, any organ or system[9]. Lum coined the phrase "fat file syndrome" to describe what we in Medical NLP refer to as the "revolving door syndrome", where patients keep returning, or move from doctor to doctor, amassing an impressive array of chronic symptoms, none of which respond to conventional treatment.

It follows, then, that helping patients to shift the pattern of breathing away from hyperventilation will not only be beneficial to overall health, but, more immediately, will also increase receptiveness to any advice, treatment or "reprogramming" that follows.

---

7 McKeown P (2005) Asthma-Free Naturally: Everything you need to know about taking control of your asthma. London:Harper Thorsons

8 Fried RZ (1986) Hyperventilation Syndrome: Research and Clinical Treatment. Johns Hopkins Series in Contemporary Medicine and Public Health

9 Lum LC (1975), hyperventilation: the tip and the iceberg, General of Psychosomatic Research, Vol. 19, pp. 375 to 383, Oxford:Pergamon Press

Increasing coherence

The correct breathing pattern is the quickest, most effective and most easily measured way of improving what some researchers now refer to as cardiac coherence. "Coherence", in this context, refers to increased synchronisation between the two branches of the autonomic nervous system, a shift in autonomic balance toward heightened parasympathetic activity, increased heart-brain synchronisation, improved vascular resonance, and entrainment between diverse physiological oscillatory systems[10]. Some of the markers of coherent functioning include a sense of emotional and physical well-being, behavioural flexibility and improved cognitive performance.

Many breathing exercises exist which purport to have beneficial value, but the easiest to learn focuses on a simple relationship between the in- and out-breaths. Put simply, the in-breath increases sympathetic functioning of the nervous system, while the out-breath activates the parasympathetic response. A slightly prolonged out-breath, then, triggers a sense of calm alertness, conducive to attentive listening, improved understanding, and greater adherence to new instructions and advice. Both in-breath and out-breath should be through the nostrils.

Even a brief period of this kind of mindful attention on the breathing pattern can have a far-reaching impact on the subject's well-being. Try this for yourself.

---

10 McCratey R, Atkinson M, Tomasino D, Bradley RT. The Coherent Heart: Heart-Brain Interactions, Psychophysiological Coherence, and the Emergence of System-Wide Order. Boulder Creek, Ca: The Institute of HeartMath

Sit comfortably and take your pulse. Ideally, it should not be much more than 70 bpm.

Now, take a small breath through the nostrils, and then breathe out. The out-breath should be somewhat longer than the in-breath. Find a comfortable ratio of in-to-out, and then take three to five breaths, keeping the rhythm as smooth as possible.
Check your pulse again, and you should notice a significant slowing down of your heart-rate.

Three steps to learning and change
The methodology for effective formatting, then, is:
1 Reduce autonomic overload by mindful attention to breathing
2 Sequence and install the new pattern
3 Test.

1. Reduce Autonomic Overload
This can be done in one of two ways:
First, the patient may be overtly coached to alter his or her breathing pattern. For example, the practitioner might say, "Just before we begin (this reduces the patient's performance anxiety), let's take a few minutes to relax. Take a normal breath in through the nose – not too deep – then slowly let it out, making sure the out-breath is just a little longer than the in-breath."

Guide the patient into a rhythm that is easy and comfortable, and then instruct the patient to take three to five more breaths following this pattern. Second, the patient may be covertly primed into the new pattern by example.

Looking directly at the patient, the practitioner should take a breath through the nose; breathe out, a few seconds longer than the in-breath, then nod, barely perceptibly, to the patient. It may take several rounds before the patient entrains to the practitioner's breathing pattern. It is important that the practitioner doesn't speak during this period of entrainment.

2. Sequence and Install the New Pattern.

One of the important messages of this chapter is that patients do not necessarily know how to get better – or, to put it differently, they may lack the solution-oriented neurological pathways necessary for change. Also, we emphasise that any new neural paths need to be activated, preferably several times (conditioning), in order to function automatically. As the famous Hebb's Postulate has it, "neurons that fire together wire together".[11]

The new pathways and a mechanism to set them in motion may be installed as follows:

1 Divide instructions into several (three to five) distinct steps.
2 Outline each step clearly.
3 Ask a question that can be answered only after the patient has mentally run through the necessary steps.

Take as an example the group of balance-assisting exercise instructions often given to a patient diagnosed with labyrinthitis (inner ear disturbance):

11 This famous phrase is usually attributed to Carla Shatz of Stanford University. See Doidge, Norman (2007). The Brain That Changes Itself. United States: Viking Press. pp. 427

1 Take a look at the instruction sheet.
2 As you can see, the exercises are simple … (run through each exercise in the correct order).
3 And you need to do them regularly five times a day for the next four weeks so you can start feeling better.

Question: Now, take a moment to think about it, then decide when you think would be the best times of day for you to do them all?

After the question has been asked, be sure you allow the patient time to consider his or her response.

3. Test
Ask the patient to review the new behavior/ response, making sure that the response is positive and congruent. Two important advantages of this methodology are:

- It is conversational.
- It by-passes analysis by the dominant brain hemisphere.

To summarize the full methodology:
1 Reduce autonomic overload; increase coherence (without this, cognitive processing will be impaired)
2 Be very explicit about what you want the patient to experience or do
3 Break the sequence down to three to five (preferably five) discrete steps and walk the patient through each of the steps in detail – e.g. "First you'll be doing (or, experiencing) A, then you'll be doing B, then you'll be doing C" etc
4 Then ask a question that can only be answered if

the patient mentally runs the sequence of actions, behaviors or experiences.

This last part requires some thought and careful design – for example, "Now you know you'll need to take one tablet every eight hours with a glass of water and on an empty stomach. What time will you need to take the first one so you can take them all and can still have a relatively undisturbed night?"

Effectively applied, this process creates and installs what might be thought of as a "future memory" – a familiar pattern into which the patient can comfortingly and effortlessly enter. As the practitioner, your responsibility is to help the patient cross the threshold from conscious to unconscious behavior, thereby increasing both concordance and adherence and optimizing the patient's progress towards recovery and ongoing health.[12]

---

12 For further information about Medical NLP, training and related topics, go to: www.medicalnlp.com and www.magicinpractice.com

NLP And Coaching

Alessio Roberti
© 2012 Alessio Roberti

One of the primary features of Coaching is its proactive, goal-oriented approach. If Coaching has become so popular since its inception in the early 1970s, it is because the idea of staying rooted in the present while focusing on your future goals and plans actually works. Therefore, once you've helped your client establish a direction by working on their vision, the next logical step is that of taking a closer look to their immediate priorities.

In this chapter, I wanted to bring together what, in my opinion, is the very best of both worlds. The GROW model originally developed by Sir John Whitmore and his colleagues, expanded with my ideas, and the well-formed outcome model, which is one of the best models that NLP has to offer when it comes to defining your goals.

Once you combine and apply these two models, you will have laid the foundation for the entire Coaching relationship. Any other issue your client might want or need to address will find its place it this broader frame of reference.

The GROW model
Coaching is ultimately about:
- Defining your client's desired outcomes.
- Assessing the present situation, in order to understand where the client stands in relation to those goals.
- Identifying what possible routes they could take, in order to get to the desired destination.

- Choosing, among these options, the most promising and practical ones, in order to transform them into an effective action plan.

These four steps are the foundation of the GROW model, an acronym that stands for:
- Goal.
- Reality.
- Options.
- What, who, when.

Goal
If you want to get anywhere in life, knowing where you want to go is of the essence.
The destination is the best place to start from, because if you begin with your dreams and aspirations then you free your mind from lots of limitations.
Quite simply, follow the steps you find in the next section of the book, and you'll have your wellformed outcome ready for the next step: Reality.

Reality
Explore the present situation together with your client. Have them talk about the here and now in relation to where they want to get. Here are some questions you can ask:
- How is the present situation different from your desired outcome?
- How is it similar?
- What are the possible obstacles that may get in your way?
- What kind of resources do you need and which do you already have?

If your client has concerns about the present situation, let them give voice to their feelings. Pace the current situation, with all it implies, and keep in mind that you're the Coach. You're not just there to listen to them, but to help them keep their eyes on the prize. You'll want them to acknowledge their issues, and then to start focusing on the possible solutions and on the better aspects of their reality.

Here are a couple more questions that will help them get back on track:
- Is this concern of yours something you can control in any way?
- Is there anything you can do to overcome this difficulty or turn it to your advantage?
- In your current situation, what are the positive aspects you're not focusing on just yet?
- Which aspects of your present situation are relevant and useful to the advancement of your objectives?
- Is there another point of view you haven't considered yet?
- Are you forgetting about something or someone?

Assessing one's own resources is also part of the getting in touch with reality process. One of NLP's principles is that people have available all the mental and emotional resources they need even if they do not currently recognize this. The Coach is there to remind them of this and to help the clients to focus on the resources.

Here are five categories your client should keep in mind when assessing their resources:
- Objects (computer, specific tools, office, etc.).
- People (family, friends, colleagues, other networks).

- Role models (acquaintances, charismatic figures).
- Knowledge (books, education, training programs, etc.).
- Personal qualities (talents, determination, charisma, etc.).
- Financial assets (already in their possession or that they could have access to).

Help your client think out of the box. How?
Perhaps they don't know how to do something, but they know someone who knows someone. They might lack the strength to achieve something all by themselves, but they might know someone who would be interested in getting to the same place (for the same or for any other reason). Should your client realize they have a problem with someone and that this is somewhat limiting their chances to success, use NLP skills to help them handle difficult relationships. Sticking to the "here and now" has the effect of allowing your client's goal to take root in reality. While you say it, it will begin to grow and shoot toward the sky. And suddenly you'll realize your client is already transitioning to the next phase: Options.

Options
At this point, if you did the previous steps, your client should already be rolling with it. The more you look at what is there, while keeping focused on the goal, the easier it is to just get one idea after another.
In order to help the transition from reality to option thinking, here are four simple questions, that I use in my daily practice, that will most certainly set the creativity wheels in motion:
- What should you start doing to reach your goal?

- What should you stop doing?
- What should you do more of?
- What should you do less of?

As a further aid to help your client let their imagination run away with them, here are some tips for a brainstorming session.[1]

Four rules for brainstorming:
- Focus on quantity, no quality. Encourage your client to keep coming up with new ideas, and avoid hesitating to put in your two cents worth, as long as it keeps the ball rolling. Instead of telling your client to be daring, sounding like a preacher, just come out with daring ideas yourself. This is the perfect occasion to practice leading by example.
- No criticizing. Any evaluation on the feasibility of the different ideas must be postponed to a later moment.
- Encourage out-of-the-box thinking. No idea is too strange or extravagant. It is easier to find the optimal solution by refining a far-fetched idea than it is to come up with a ready-made final solution.
- Let old ideas breed new ideas. Combine them, add to them, make any sort of change. Toying and tinkering with what you have often leads to unexpectedly good results. Generating options is about creativity. This isn't the time to make a choice, yet. And there's no need to try and be "reasonable" or "realistic". With this I'm not saying that your client should only go after silly or seemingly unreasonable ideas, but the fact is that the best solutions are often invisible to the

1 If you deem it advisable to do some in-depth work on creativity related issues, read the fantastic book Thinkertoys by Michael Michalko for further insight.

eye, at first. And great ideas often come after toying for a while with what seemed impossible at first!

Selecting options, on the other hand, is pretty much about realism, yet of a creative kind. In order to narrow down the choice, instead of just having them reject the wacky ideas, take some time to explore each option "as if" that was the final decision. Tell your client to assume their job was to make the impossible possible, and ask the following questions:

- How could you make this work?
- What does this idea miss to be perfect?
- Which downsides represent an obstacle you must remove?
- What other options do not present this drawback, or would help you solve it?
- How could you make the two options blend into a new and better solution?

Help your client refine their ideas and narrow the options down until they get to one or two viable courses of action.

What, who, when
The final step of the GROW model is as much straightforward as it is vital to the actualization of any outcome. If you never get to decide what needs to be done and when, your goals – well-formed as they may be – will remain just pretty fantasies.
What you need to do now is:

- Break down the process into steps (the "what").
- Find out when they're going to happen and, if

necessary, who's going to be involved.
- Focus on the very first step: the one thing your client can do right now to build momentum and really get things started.

Breaking down the process is particularly important when you have complex or long-term projects. Having a succession of simpler steps ensures that your client:

- Focuses on something they can surely manage.
- Always knows exactly what to do (and what to do next).
- Takes notice of the passing of time.
- Receives continuous feedback as to the right course of action.
- Stays motivated by completing the different steps, successfully.

Here are some questions you can ask in order to bring the attention on the important issues.

- What will you do?
- When will you do it? And how long will it take?
- Who needs to know?
- How would you like me to hold you accountable?
- What obstacles could come in your way?
- How will you overcome them?
- What is the very first step you will take, now?

Create a one page template for yourself. And it's on one page for several good reasons. Longer lists tend to kill motivation, and all people ever do with a bunch of sheets of paper is pile them up, put them on a side, and forget all about them. Instead, what you want your client to do is to keep focused for the days and weeks to come. A single-page action plan can be kept in full view where your client is most likely to see it (next to their PC, on the fridge, on the bathroom mirror, as a wallpaper for their laptop), so that it works as a constant reminder. And talking about motivation, it is essential that the goal comes first and that it's written in a language that is both concise and appealing. Otherwise all you have is a list of chores: had they been appealing in and of themselves, your client wouldn't have come to you in the first place! Be essential and keep it simple: you don't need to put on paper every single little step. Just enough to put your client at ease: they should feel that they can do it, and have a clear sense of what is up and coming.

"Everything should be made as simple as possible, but no simpler."

Albert Einstein

As a last step, check for motivation. Just ask your client:
· On a scale from 0 to 10, how motivated do you feel to jump into action?

If the level is seven or less, you need to retrace your steps and get it to a solid eight, at the very least. Use your instincts or ask your client what they think could be improved. Remember that whatever response you get is just a feedback: if the motivation is not there yet, it might very well be that there are some issues you need to work on. Stay open and curious about what is going on. This is an unprecedented opportunity for your client to come to grips with something that could really make the difference in their life.

Well-formed outcomes

Any Coach would agree on the fact that setting clear goals for your client is of the essence. The advantage of bringing NLP into the mix is that it tells you exactly how to do it. Being one of the most popular models in the NLP world, it has been presented in many different variations, but eventually it always boils down to the outcome having these six qualities:

- Positive.
- Desirable.
- Sensory-based.
- Time-framed.
- Self-started and self-maintained.
- Ecological.

Positive

The word "positive", here, is used as a synonym to "affirmative". In other words, your client should be clear as to what they want, instead of what they don't want. So the first thing you want to ask your client is simply:
- What do you want, specifically?

Watch out for words such as "stop", "quit", or "tired of". Even though an answer such as "I want to quit smoking" contains no negation, it still states what the client doesn't want: smoking. These kind of answers are actually quite frequent, especially with clients who have an "away from" preference in their Meta-program direction. Acknowledge their needs – after all, being

tired of one's old job is as good a starting point as any –
and keep focusing on the desired outcome by asking:
• And what do you want, instead?

The bottom line is that no matter what your client
wants to "get rid of" or "stop doing", eventually they'll
still have to come up with something different that their
brain can focus on and work with.

Desirable

Many would claim that clients need a thousand reasons
to get motivated enough. As much as I agree on the
fact that adding new reasons can only increase the
level of motivation, what I truly believe is that you don't
need a thousand reasons – one is more than plenty, if
it's the right one. When it comes to motivation, there's
an important distinction we need to make right away.
On the one hand, you have the goals your client wants
to and is actually eager to pursue. On the other, the
goals your client feels they ought to pursue, but when
they think about doing it, their response is less than
enthusiastic.

With the goals they want to pursue, you can just go on
and ask this one simple question:
• Why is this goal important to you?

Whatever answer they give you, just feed it back to
them and ask:
• And why is this important to you?
Do that a couple more times and you will have done
your client a great service.
For starters, this is a motivation booster – which is
exactly what you wanted in the first place. Second, this

kind of questioning highlights possible discrepancies between the desired or imagined effect of having reached the goal, and the actual possible consequences of pursuing it. Imagine your client wants to start their own business, and that the reason why they want to do it is to have more freedom. But then, since they don't have the cash, they're going to team up with a partner, and this could end up being an even greater limit to their freedom. Make sure they give the matter enough thought – there's still plenty of time to revise that initial goal. Third, finding the actual reason why your client wants to do a certain thing opens the doors to a wealth of new possibilities. Once you know your client is after freedom, you might ask how they would measure it. Perhaps all they need to feel "free" is a shabby hut in the forest where they can go whenever they want and just "be themselves".

Last, if you couldn't get a positive outcome with the previous step, there's a good chance you can at least get a positive reason for that. Go with it and see where it takes you.

Ask a question along these lines:
- Is there something you could actively do, instead, to bring more (insert motivation here) into your life?

With the things your client feels they ought to do, things are somewhat different. The point being that here they probably already have a long list of good reasons why they should do it, and they end up not doing it anyway. So, instead of asking why that goal is important, we're going to go the other way around.

Let me first give you an example, and then we'll look into it.

Coach: So, tell me what you want.

Client: I want to become a regular at my gym.

Coach: It feels like you've been trying this already, and it didn't work out.

Client: True. I've made this decision before, but then I don't follow through.

Coach: Ok. And why do you think that is? What stops you from exercising regularly?

Client: I always seem to find at least one good reason not to go, after all. And, honestly? It hurts! It hurts when I'm there, and it hurts even worse the day after.

Coach: So there are plenty of things you would rather do and it hurts.

Client: Sure.

Coach: And, tell me, what would be the one thing that would make you forget about those other things and go regularly, even though it hurts?

Client: Mmhh… I guess if I found out that I have a condition, if my health depended on it.

Coach: And if your health depended on it, you're sure you'd follow through.

Client: Absolutely.

Coach: Good. And now consider this: is there something else, in your life, that would make you put aside even this commendable concern for your health?

Client: Probably my family. They would always come first.

Coach: Have you got kids?

Client: Two boys.

Coach: And you want to be a good role model for them?

Client: Yeah!
Coach: And how important would you say this is for you?
Client: I'm beginning to see where you're heading to with this. And I must say I like it…

When the drive for not doing something is greater than the drive for doing it, first you need to know what you're up against. Basically the Coach here was looking for counter examples – things that would make you reconsider your position. So, if it's something they would do, you look for something that would make them stop doing it. If it's something they wouldn't do, you look for something that would make them start doing it. This works because our values – our reasons why – are not all on the same level. There is a hierarchy and by asking these questions you make your way to the top.

Once you have a high level value, you have your "right" reason. Then all you need to do is find a way to bring this kind of motivation into the desired outcome. And the simplest way to go about it is by asking your client how they would do it.

Sensory-based

By now, it's common knowledge: goals need to be specific. What common knowledge will not tell you is how to make it happen. In fact, I would go as far as claiming that "being specific" is a very unspecific statement, and that's why, in the NLP world, we prefer talking about goals having a sensory-based representation. Simply put, your client will have to find the answer to the question:

- What specifically will you see, hear, and feel, when you have achieved this goal?

A full sensory-based representation of the desired outcome has two major positive effects. First, it will give your client a reference experience that will let them know they have arrived, when they finally get there. Second, it ensures that their other mind "gets it". It's a conscious effort to communicate with one's own brain in the simplest way possible – using the brain's own language. What books usually forget to mention, though, is that in order to benefit from both effects, your client needs to look at thing from two different points of view.

In the first case, your client will need a fully associated experience – that is, they need to see what they would see if they actually were living the moment, hear what they would hear, and feel exactly what they would feel. They need to be able to recognize the experience from "within themselves". On the other hand, if they keep experiencing their goal "as if" they had gotten it already, their brain will fall for it, and it will stop trying to achieve it. What they need, instead, is a role model – a living image of themselves as they will look, move, talk, dress, and so on, once they get there. Seeing themselves from the outside is what will make their brain want to go for it. It's a subtle difference, but it's fundamental for getting in the right state of mind.

A double perspective
1 Focus on your goal, and imagine what you will see, hear, and feel, specifically, once you achieve it.
2 Allow yourself to fully experience what it means to

have it right here, right now. Look around you: what do you see? (Pause after each question.) What do you hear? How do you feel? What do you see around you that reminds you of your achievement? Focus on some of the most remarkable details. Take all the time that you need to let the experience sink in, and be with you for future reference.

3 Now take some distance from it all. Just enough so that you can see yourself in there. How do you look? How do you move? How do you talk? What are the reminders of the fact that you made it? Who's with you? What are you doing?

4 Take a good look at the whole scene, and in particular at yourself. In fact, take a snapshot, or a video – something to remember it by. Make sure that the picture is big, colorful, and bright enough to keep you going for it.

Time-framed
Having a well-defined, sensory-specific goal is not enough. If you never put it in your time-line, it's rare that it's going to happen. Setting a time frame is what actually transforms a dream into a plan. So make sure your client puts a time stamp in their definition of the goal. Another good idea is breaking the whole thing down into more manageable chunks and set a time frame for each part. You can either do it at this stage, or wait until you get to work on your client's action plan, in the final phase of the GROW model.

Self-started and self-maintained
A goal can be perfect in any other aspect, and still be totally and utterly out of your client's control.
"Inheriting a million dollars from the rich aunt you've

never known about within the next 12 months" is
a outcome that your client can do nothing at all to
achieve. And that is a no-no.
"Winning the New York Lottery within the next 12
months" is a little bit better: at least it's self-started!

But they still have no saying in the matter, once they
bought their ticket. What you want your client to do is
to devise a goal that is within their sphere of influence.
And if it involves other people, your client should focus
on what they themselves can do in order to stir things
in the right direction.
"I want her to love me" is a recipe for disaster. "I want
to become the kind of person that she (or, even better,
that someone like her) would fall in love with" is still
somewhat vague, but it sure sound healthier.

Ecological
The final and possibly the most important step to a
well-defined outcome. In NLP, ecological means "in
balance with the rest of the person's life". If in order to
pursue a certain goal your client needs to give up their
career for good, quarrel with their friends or lose their
health over it, the goal is not ecological. What you need
to do is establish the context and see how the goal fits
into the "bigger scheme" of things.
Most things in life are desirable at certain times and
in certain situations, and undesirable under other
circumstances. "Raising one's energy level" is a good
idea when you want to be energized, but do you really
want to feel like that all day and all night? How long do
you think you could go without sleeping?

So here are three simple questions for your client:

- When, where and with whom do you want it?
- When, where and with whom do you not want it?
- Is there a time and place where having this outcome would prove unwelcome?

As for the second aspect of an ecological outcome, your client needs to consider that everything comes with a price. Pursuing a goal takes time, energy, possibly money: all things they might have to subtract from some other aspect of their life. I'm saying "might have", because it doesn't necessarily have to be an either/or choice. Taking time for yourself doesn't need to be something you actually do all by yourself; eating healthy food doesn't need to be "boring"; and working for a better future doesn't have to make your present hell!

You need to address the issue, and you can do it by asking the following questions:

- Pursuing this goal will have a cost, financial and otherwise. Do you find your goal is worth the price?
- Pursuing this goal will take up part of your time, time you might have to subtract to something else. Do you find your goal is worth your time?
- Is there something in the present situation that you're not ready or willing to give up?
- Achieving this goal will bring changes in your life: what you do, who you spend your time with, how you see yourself, how others see you. Are you positive that this is a fully desirable outcome?

This would be an excellent time to use your calibration skills and check for congruence. Don't take your client's word as gospel truth – use your sensory acuity and make sure their non-verbal cues are congruent with what they say. Raising ecological issues might bring the goal definition process to a halt. Instead of giving up the dream, help your client integrate the different aspects into a better-defined goal. Give it a fair chance, but if your client eventually realizes that the different instances are irreconcilable, it is better to stop now, than to head unwarily for disaster.

At this point your client should have formed a goal that is positive, desirable, stated in sensory-specific terms, time-framed, self-started, self-sustained and ecological. Bring it within the frame of the GROW model, and your client's desires will have more chances to become solid realities.

How to set your goals: from dream to reality

GROW
1 Goal: establish where you want to go (apply rules for well-formed outcomes).
2 Reality: assess current situation (in relation to the goal, complete with concerns, and resources).
3 Options: scout possible routes (broad choice first, then work towards an optimal solution).
4 What, who, when: design action plan (follow the template).

Well-formed outcomes
1 Positive: What do you want?
2 Desirable: Why is it important to you?

3 Sensory-based: What specifically will you see, hear, and feel, when you have achieved this goal?
4 Time-framed: When will it happen?
5 Self-started and self-maintained: Is it under your control? Is it under your influence?
6 Ecological: When, where and with whom do you want it? When, where and with whom do you not want it? Is it worth the price, time, and effort?

Tips and tricks
Check always for congruence (or the lack thereof) and have your client tell you about any strange or "off" feelings they might experience, as these probably address the questions of desirability and ecology. Remember to use the pillars of NLP: rapport, flexibility and sensory acuity. All this said, remember that these frameworks may very well be the perfect chance for you, Coach, to get your own goals straight as well!

Changing Beliefs

Owen Fitzpatrick & Alessio Roberti

Our beliefs are at the core of our being and extremely important for our life because they guide every behavior and decision. They determine what we regard as possible and what we imagine as out of our reach. Some of our beliefs are not "completely" our own. We blindly take them from others. The problem is that, once a belief is formed, we just act on it. Even if the belief is something limiting like "Nobody likes me" or "I am not a people person."

In this module we want to explore three main concepts:

1 How come we let our beliefs govern us, even if they damage us or the people we care for?
2 How beliefs work and why they are so important.
3 Can we consciously make changes to what we believe?

In the first half of the 20th century the world believed that it was impossible to run a mile under four minutes. When, on May 6th 1954, Roger Bannister ran a mile in 3 min 59.4 seconds, everyone was in awe. The belief that a 4-minute mile run was impossible was destroyed. Within a few years many other runners broke the four minute barrier. It was as if a spell had been broken. To understand this phenomenon better, we have to take a closer look at what we consider to be the most important subject you can study: belief systems.

It's our beliefs that tell us what we can or cannot achieve, what goals we should consider possible, or how worthy we are of other people's acceptance. Because of their restrictive nature, these beliefs are usually known as "Limiting Beliefs". They typically sound like "I will never be successful", "People don't like me", "I can't…", etc.

There are three types of limiting beliefs we'd like to start by looking at:

- Hopelessness: My goal cannot be reached under any circumstances.
- Helplessness: My goal can be reached, but I lack something to achieve it and I'll never find it.
- Worthlessness: I don't deserve to achieve this goal, because of something that I am (or that I'm not) or because of something that I have (or that I haven't) done.

In order to uncover these types of beliefs, you can ask questions like:

- In case of Hopelessness: Why is this goal unreachable?
- In case of Helplessness: What do you lack to reach it?
- In case of Worthlessness: Why don't you deserve to achieve this goal?

Listen carefully to the answers, and you will uncover the limiting "reasons" that stand between people and their goals. Now, in NLP, sometimes you might hear that you should never ask Why and indeed when you are looking to challenge a belief Why isn't very useful but in this case it helps you by exploring the person's 'theories' which will often reveal their limiting beliefs which you want to get at in the first place. Once you, and the person you work with, "become aware" of these limiting beliefs and reasons, as Richard Bandler says: the door of opportunity opens.

Furthermore, beliefs are built by us taking what we experience and filtering it through our previous held beliefs so that we develop new beliefs based on old ones. For example, if you believe all English people are a certain way, then every time you meet an English person,, you will filter your experience of meeting them by looking for the quality that 'English people' possess in your mind. This can be problematic because we tend to want to be right all the time and so often we will dismiss evidence that contradicts our beliefs and we will instead accept only evidence that supports them.

What this means is that we can develop pretty strong beliefs over time because, as Robert Anton Wilson, author of Quantum Psychology, explains, whatever the thinker thinks, the prover proves. In other words, in our mind we have a part that comes up with ideas and a part that looks for evidence to prove we are correct about these ideas. The part that looks for evidence will dismiss any evidence that doesn't serve it. So, we get lost by allowing our beliefs determine how we experience events. This can have a catastrophic impact on our life. If you believe that you are stupid then you might never try to improve your potential and thus never achieve a goal that might well be in your reach. If you believe the recession is impossible to overcome, you might well quit your business even if you have a chance to turn it around.

So the importance of learning about your limiting beliefs cannot and should not be underestimated. The most important thing you can do is to take control over what you believe because it will help ensure you are really living up to your potential. Many, many times people fall short because they don't believe enough in themselves. They believe they can't change, that no one can help them and that they don't deserve to change. Help them change that and you change their world.

Changing Beliefs
Once you understand the critical need for working effectively with beliefs, the next question is how do you actually change beliefs? Well, NLP and in particular Richard Bandler's work offers us some extremely useful skills that we can use to change beliefs. Beliefs are ideas that we have a sense of certainty about. As such, one way to change beliefs is to create a feeling of doubt and connect it with the other persons belief. Next, the key would be to propose a new, more resourceful belief and attach a feeling of certainty to it.

So, with the NLP model of submodalities you can find out from a person when they think about things that they doubt, what are the submodalities. Once you do this, you can then ask them when they think of things they are certain about what are the submodalities. The next phase is the cool part. Then you can have them imagine taking the Limiting Belief they have and moving it into the same submodalities of doubt. And you can have them take the new resourceful belief that they want instead and get them to imagine moving that into the same submodalities as what they feel certain about. By doing so, you help them to start to doubt the limiting belief and start to feel more certain about the resourceful belief.

Belief Change Technique:

1 Elicit the submodalities for doubt
2 Elicit the submodalities for certainty
3 Think of the limiting belief that you have
4 Think of the resourceful belief that you want to believe instead
5 Imagine the limiting belief moving into the submodalities for doubt
6 Imagine the resourceful belief moving into the submodalities for certainty

Meta Model Questions
Another useful skill in helping people change beliefs is the Meta Model. The Meta Model is a set of questions that allow us to specify and clarify information and by doing so, help open up their map of the world.
When we build our beliefs we do so by having experiences and then extracting meaning from the experiences. The Meta Model helps us to expand our map or model of the world so that we get to the realization that maybe these beliefs are not as correct as we think they are.

So, for example, if you believe that 'There is no hope, I can't change' we might ask you 'What stops you?' and you might respond 'Because I don't know how'. We can then ask you 'What would happen if you learned how to change?' At this point, you'd be likely to explain what 'would' happen and as soon as you can imagine it in your mind it makes it far more realistic a possibility. Or if you were to say 'People just can't help me.' we might ask you 'Who specifically can't help you?' or 'How exactly can't they help you?'. By doing so, as soon as you identify the person that you say 'can't help you' we might continue and ask how you know they can't? or what do you mean by they can't?

What will happen is that you were be forced to be very specific over what experience has led you to the conclusion that no one can help you and of course at this stage you won't be able to argue the merits of the question. Another example is if you said 'I'm worthless and I don't deserve a good life' we might ask 'How do you know?' and you might respond 'Because I keep trying and failing'. We can then ask you 'How does the fact that you tried and failed in the past MEAN that you're worthless and don't deserve a good life?' At this point after just two questions it's hard to continue holding your limiting belief because the logic behind it is inherently flawed.

Some powerful Meta Mode Questions:

- How do you know?
- What do you mean?
- Who says?
- Compared to Who?
- What/Who/When/Where/How Specifically?
- What stops you?
- What would happen if you could?

Milton Model Patterns

The Milton Model is a set of language patterns that allow us to create rapport with another person and lead them toward believing what we believe. It helps us to build a belief in another person's mind indirectly. It's often described as hypnotic language. Two particular patterns in the Milton Model that are useful to understand are Truisms and Presuppositions. For our purposes, Truisms are when you say something that is true for the person you are talking to. By saying what they are thinking or something they agree with, you ensure that it will be easier to influence them.

Presuppositions are an incredibly powerful tool in influence. When you presuppose something instead of saying it you are embedding it more powerfully in their mind. So, instead of saying... This module is really easy to understand... we might say... before you realize just why this module is so easy to understand. The second way is far more powerful because we are assuming it as obviously true rather than suggesting it overtly.

So, if you are talking to someone who feels hopeless, helpless and worthless then you can start by saying 'I understand that sometimes life can seem hopeless and like there's nothing you can do. Sometimes it's easy to feel like you don't deserve a good life (to pace their experience with truisms) and when you realize that these feelings were masking the truth you will discover that you can change and you can get help. How much you will improve is up to you but no matter how quickly you find yourself feeling really good, you'll notice that after all of the great things you have done in your life, the reason you deserve it so much is because you've done your best so often.' (plenty of presuppositions highlighted by italics assuming what you want them to believe)

Sleight of Mouth Patterns
Sleight of Mouth Patterns are an extension of the Meta Model. They represent a number of language patterns that challenge limiting beliefs by helping the person see the beliefs in a different way. Without going in depth on them, some basics are challenging the generalization by exaggerating or specifying or giving a counter example. For example, when someone says the belief 'I'm hopeless and can never change' you could say 'So, if you are driving into a wall you can't even change direction... or you can't change clothes?' By making what they said exaggerated they will often have to clarify and by doing so the belief itself will open up some more. So, they will be specific and therefore less limiting. Or you could specify by saying something like 'Which part of you exactly is hopeless and which things specifically can't you change?' By doing this you nit-pick and get them realizing that when they chunk it down to this level the belief again doesn't work.

Or you could simply say 'Has there ever been anything that you could change?' asking them for one counter example that challenges the generalization directly. Another pattern is changing the meaning which is like reframing. In this case when they say 'Nobody can help me to change because I'm completely lost' you could rephrase the belief back to them and say 'So, you haven't yet found anyone to help you change because you're not 100% clear over where you are right now?' By rephrasing it like this you open up the belief so that they have more possibilities inside of it.

These are just some of the amazing tools we have in NLP at our disposal to help ourselves and others change beliefs. When you are trying to help someone before even using the technique to help them overcome a phobia or become happier or more confident, it might be useful to help them believe that they can change, that they will change and that the change will last. Probably one of the most important changes in beliefs that they need to have is in their identity or the beliefs that they have about themselves. When they believe that they are a certain kind of person, that belief will determine what behaviors they engage in. For example, a person who sees themselves as a smoker will never quit smoking for good as it's not who they are in their mind. Once they are able to see themselves as a non-smoker they can then change what they do on a regular basis because it fits in with their identity.

So, in conclusion, beliefs are important to work with because they determine our behaviors and dictate how we experience the world. When you take control over your beliefs, you will find yourself transforming your world. There are many skills, models and techniques that can help you change your beliefs such as the submodality belief change to the Meta model questions and Milton model patterns as well as the sleight of mouth patterns. By combining these approaches you will find yourself extremely effective at bringing about change.

The beliefs of hopelessness, helplessness and worthlessness are among the most important beliefs to work with and if you can use your skills to help people realize that there is hope in their future and they can change; that they can get help and find the solution; and that they do deserve it because of the kind of person they are, their identity... then you will have done them a great service.

Strategies for Learning

Kate Benson

Until the creation of NLP there was no really systematic way of working out the elegant, efficient, or effective way to learn something new. Fortunately we now have the tools to do this, so we can train ourselves and others to optimize the process of learning. This chapter introduces the some of the key process in learning strategies so you can begin to elicit and install really great strategies to learn new things for yourself and for others.

Human beings are learning machines. From the day we are born, and perhaps even before we are born, the human baby is learning. We are hard wired for learning. Most people have learned the two most difficult and important skills before anyone even thinks of sending them to school. These are talking and walking. Imagine if you had to break down either of these skills into tiny stages, step by step, to write the talking and walking manual. How complicated and difficult would that be? Yet the majority of people manage to learn these skills easily. Later as we grow into older children and adults we are told to 'learn' something. Learn to read, learn to spell, learn to do mathematics and we want to gain a myriad of skills and knowledge. Fortunately many people manage to figure out a way to do this. It may not be the best or most efficient way of doing so but as resourceful learning machines we figure out how 'learn' something new.

The first challenge we face is the word 'learn'. This is a relatively nominalized verb. The steps and processes taken or needed to achieve the learning are unspecified. What exactly is the person supposed to do? How do they start? How do they know when to stop? We can break this nominalized verb down into a few smaller chunks by instructing someone to remember, read, calculate but it really doesn't move us much further on because we still don't know what to do on the inside of our heads. Most of the instructions relate to what we are told to do on the outside.

Effective learning strategies must specify exactly what a person needs to do on the inside of their brain and in their bodies to effectively learn something new. There are a number of ways to work this out. The easy way to find out which strategies are the most elegant and effective is to find someone who has learned the skill and is brilliant at it. We then use a process of elicitation to discover the steps the person goes through to learn the skill. Then it is simply a matter of giving the learner, whether this is yourself or another person the steps to do inside their own heads. Alternatively we can find out what the person is doing that isn't working and change it so that it does work by altering some aspect of their current strategy. Finally we can design a perfect strategy from scratch. The ability to learn something really effectively involves more than simply the steps to learning. The learning strategy encompasses the range of skills, attitudes and beliefs that make up the field of NLP which can and do come into play when helping someone learn really well.

A great learner:
- Has a strong belief that he or she can and will learn.
- Gets into just the right state to engage in the learning.

- Knows when to begin learning.
- Has the right motivational strategy.
- Knows exactly the steps to go through in their mind to learn the particular subject or skill.
- Uses possible setbacks to build propulsion to motivate themselves even more.
- Knows when they are finished and have achieved what they set out to do.
- Feels really great about their achievement so that competence builds confidence.

In other chapters in this book there are many strategies and suggestions for creating just the right state and for changing beliefs, so in this chapter we will concentrate on the key factors involved in great learning and trust that you will apply what you learn in the other chapters to learning exquisitely.

The strong belief and right state for learning depends in part on what you want to learn. Some states are conducive to great learning, such as curiosity, fun, motivation and even frustration sometimes helps. Discovering how someone creates the perfect state for learning can be extremely precise and wonderfully elegant. One of my students Helen is a voracious reader; she is extremely fast and has a very high retention rate for information. She is as happy reading a technical report as she is reading a novel. I know a lot of readers who don't enjoy reading and do so inefficiently so I was keen to discover her strategy. It turns out her strategy isn't very unusual but how she creates her state for reading is very unique.

When she thinks of reading she smells a mixture of aftershave and pipe smoke! Her father sat her on his knee each night when he came home from work and read the Financial Times to her using his finger to point out the words. She has a strong anchor which associates reading with pleasure and comfort as a result.

When Helen is about to read something, she looks at it and decides on what the perfect reading room would be. If it is a report she may decide it would be best to sit on a high chair with a stainless steel desk and a strong light. If it is a novel she may decide on a comfy high back chair and a roaring fire. Once she has created her perfect reading room in her mind she sits down and starts reading. This way it doesn't matter if she is on the underground or a bus or standing in a force 7 gale she reads away happily in her room!

The simplest and most well-known strategy is the strategy for learning to spell in English. It is a useful one to start with to explain the process. Contrary to popular belief there isn't one strategy or 'THE NLP spelling strategy'. However it is possible to identify some key processes that great spellers do well and poor spellers don't do.

When we ask someone how to spell a word, good spellers will usually look up to their right, look at the word in their mind (their spelling database) and when they see it there, they get a good feeling down their midline – a positive yes! Ask a person who is OK at spelling to spell a word they will look up to their right, check it by sounding the letters out or sometimes breaking the word into phonemes and then get a positive yes. Ask a poor speller to spell a word and they will do a whole range of other things! For example they may look up to their left and discover the word isn't there, then they say to themselves 'Oh no I don't know how to spell this', then they will look down and feel bad, then they will try to work it out phonetically and finally they get a yuck feeling and are still not sure!

NLP teaches us that we 'think' by making pictures and sounds, talking to ourselves and having associated feelings. We have 5 senses which we use to experience the world and five ways to represent or re-present the world to ourselves. So when we know this we can 'Think on Purpose'! The senses we use on the inside are therefore referred to as the representational systems. The qualities of these representations or modalities are referred to as the submodalities. So for example if a speller makes a small, faint image of a word in their head it won't be as effective as a huge bright and colorful image in helping to recall the word.

The sequence for a great spelling strategy is as follows:
- See the word on the outside.
- Make a picture of the word inside your head.
- The bigger brighter and more memorable this image is the easier it is to remember.
- Match the word on the outside with the one on the inside and make sure are the same.
- Get a good feeling of certainty down the midline of your body.
- Repeat about 3 times to be sure the process is installed.

So the next time you see or write the word all you have to do is check the word on the outside is the same as the one on the inside. One lady I taught to spell during a break in a seminar was furious afterward! She angrily said: "For 40 years I thought I was stupid. Why hasn't anyone taught me this simple way of spelling before?!"

It's not that some people are naturally good at spelling and some aren't, it's that they have learned to do it in a way that doesn't work very well. It is perfectly understandable that people do these things because, as intelligent individuals, faced with the prospect of learning something new and without any guidance as to how to do it, they will work something out for themselves. Teachers and parents present spelling in same way that they have been told or believe works (this may just be the way they do it). It's inevitable that some learners get it right and others don't.

The questions to ask to elicit a learning strategy are basically the same as for any other strategy and include:
- What happens when you are learning something?
- What do you do to prepare to learn something?
- What are the steps you go through to learn something quickly?
- What do you do if you get stuck?
- What lets you know that you have finished learning something?

Often people don't consciously know what they do so it is important to look for eye accessing cues and other non-verbal cues so you can see what they are actually doing. Most effective strategies are very short, contain no unnecessary steps and have no loops. Most good strategies will have a visual, auditory and kinesthetic element within the sequence.

To explore this further, let's look at an entirely different learning process to identify how to create an effective strategy from scratch. In this instance we have to 'engineer' the strategy. This is part of the work of Design Human Engineering™ where we can create perfect strategies without relying on finding an 'expert'. Many of you will have taken non-verbal spatial reasoning tests as a child. Here is a simple example.

Which two shapes are the same?

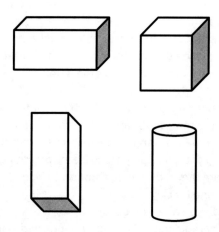

You are probably looking at this and thinking well that's easy! Of course it is when you have the correct strategy. I helped a little boy called Sam, who, although he was very bright and great at English and Maths, could not for the life of him do these types of puzzle. His teacher's advice was to keep practicing. Of course the more he practiced the more he got it wrong so he became really good at getting it wrong!

In order to answer this question the following steps are required:

1 Look at the line drawing of the first image and create, in your imagination a representation of the lines as a 3 dimensional object.

2 At the moment it is 2 parallel lines with one further off set parallel line above, 3 horizontal lines, two aligned and one offset. Plus 3 further lines joining some of the other lines. It's just a series of lines until you hallucinate something out of the lines!

3 Once you have hallucinated a shape from the lines, store this image and do the same with the other images.

4 Next rotate each image in turn and compare the image with the other images until you find two that, when rotated in a certain way, match.

5 Then flatten the two images back into line drawings on the page to identify which two are the same.

The young boy I worked with said that he didn't like Art because he had no imagination. This was a big clue to how to help him. Unless he could imagine the shape coming off the page and be able to rotate the imaginary image he would not be able to solve the problem.

The solution was clear. First he needed to exercise his imagination 'muscles' and begin to build pictures in his head. So our first 'game' was to draw music. We listened to Vivaldi's 'four Seasons' and drew the music. The second step was to 'reverse engineer' the process of solving the puzzle. We photographed a number of objects including; a cube, a tube and a rectangular box. Next we printed out the photos and traced them onto transparent paper. We had now moved 3 dimensional objects into 2 dimensional images and into line drawings. As soon as Sam experiences the process in this direction he was able to reverse the process with the line drawings and solve the puzzle.

Sam's new strategy for solving non-verbal reasoning is now:
- Have a good strong confident feeling and says to himself 'I know how to do this'.
- Feels really excited about solving the puzzle.
- Knows that this is the moment to start.
- Imagines doing the puzzle and the more he does the better he feels and the more he wants to get it right.
- Takes the line drawings and imagines them as 3D images. Rotates them and looks to see which 2 are the same.
- Puts them back to 2D and selects the correct two that are the same.
- The more he does the more confident he feels.
- Has a really satisfied feeling when he completes the puzzles.

Another key feature of effective learning strategies is knowing when to start and when to stop and to know how to motivate yourself through the tough parts. As a teacher I encounter these three factors often with students. Your average teenager can find a million other things to do rather than their homework. Other students just don't know when they are done. They are the ones who say 'I just have to redraft it one more time – it's nearly done'. They are never satisfied and are usually late with assignments. Other students just want to give up when the going gets tough.

What is needed here is a bit of obsession! Obsession to get started, obsession to keep going and an obsession to get it finished. Most teenagers are good at being obsessed with something. It is usually a game on their computer or their phones. Elicit the strategy for playing 7 hours straight on a computer game and you will discover precisely the strategy they need for motivating themselves for learning. It will look something like this:

1 Look at the computer and feel an overwhelming desire to turn it on and load the game.
2 Run the movie of exactly where you were and the obstacles that you overcame to get there.
3 Feel really satisfied with what you have done so far and imagine how even better it will feel when you beat the dragon and get to the next level.
4 Keep playing the game and every time you drop back feel propelled to try again.
5 Keep going until someone insists you go to bed.

Eventually after days of this you complete the game. Celebrate wildly leaping around the room and cheering. Then post it on Facebook to tell all your friends how you did it!
So once we have the strategy for motivation and propulsion it is just a matter of attaching it to the learning.

The process of applying a strategy from one context to a different context is to move the submodalities of motivation and apply them to the desired learning activity.
With the right strategy and the right motivation there is no reason why anyone can't learn anything they want to. Even people who have had brain injuries have re-

learnt many skills. People who have been told all their lives that they won't be able to do learn something have proved the world wrong and gone on to great things. Einstein didn't speak until he was seven. He was a slow developer but he just didn't stop once he started being curious. The brain is amazingly flexible and most of us do not use anything like the brain power we have.

So go on learn something new.

CPSIA information can be obtained at www.ICGtesting.com
Printed in the USA
LVOW06s1334080715

445434LV00017B/340/P